Winner of Parental Wisdom's Good Parenting Seal

Be Confident in Who You Are

MIDDLE SCHOOL
CONFIDENTIAL™

BOOK 1

ANNIE FOX, M.Ed.
ILLUSTRATED BY **MATT KINDT**

free spirit
PUBLISHING®

Library of Congress Cataloging-in-Publication Data
Fox, Annie, 1950–
  Be confident in who you are / Annie Fox.
    p. cm. — (Middle school confidential)
  Includes index.
  ISBN-13: 978-1-57542-302-9
  ISBN-10: 1-57542-302-2
  1. Self-confidence—Juvenile literature. 2. Middle school students—Juvenile literature. I. Title.
  BF575.S39F69 2008
  155.5'182–dc22

                                                                            2008004754

  ISBN: 978-1-57542-302-9

Free Spirit Publishing does not have control over or assume responsibility for author or third-party websites and their content. At the time of this book's publication, all facts and figures cited within are the most current available. All telephone numbers, addresses, and website URLs are accurate and active; all publications, organizations, websites, and other resources exist as described in this book; and all have been verified as of August 2021. If you find an error or believe that a resource listed here is not as described, please contact Free Spirit Publishing. Parents, teachers, and other adults: We strongly urge you to monitor children's use of the Internet.

Reading Level Grade 6; Interest Level Ages 11–14; Fountas & Pinnell Guided Reading Level Y

Edited by Douglas J. Fehlen
Cover design and illustration by Matt Kindt
Interior design by Jayne Curtis

15 14 13 12
Printed in the United States of America
V20301221

Free Spirit Publishing Inc.
6325 Sandburg Road, Suite 100
Minneapolis, MN 55427-3674
(612) 338-2068
help4kids@freespirit.com
freespirit.com

Free Spirit offers competitive pricing.
Contact edsales@freespirit.com for pricing information on
multiple quantity purchases.

Dedication

To David, always in all ways. I'm who I am today because I know you.

Acknowledgments

My own middle school memories wouldn't have sustained me through writing this book. Fortunately, I receive middle school confidential updates from students around the world. Their daily email is a source of wisdom for me and for teens and parents who visit www.anniefox.com.

Thank you to Matt Kindt for his brilliant illustrations. Without his creativity, the character narratives would just be words on a page. Hats off to Jayne Curtis for her dynamic design. Jayne's creativity between these covers has been a wonderful asset. I'm also most appreciative of the ongoing support of Judy Galbraith, John Kober, and the team at Free Spirit. To my editor, Douglas Fehlen, goes a huge thank you and a big hug. His enthusiasm for this series was obvious from the start. His input throughout the "structural organization" was invaluable. Douglas's special ability to listen with respect and offer feedback has nurtured me and this process for many months.

Thanks also to: my daughter, Fayette, for always being so interested in my work; my son, Ezra, and his girlfriend, Sarah Jebrock, for the many insightful conversations about middle school social dynamics; Whitman friends, Alex and Chris, for providing a philosophy major's spin on adolescence; and the helpful YA librarians at San Rafael Public Library.

Finally, I'd like to thank my sweet husband and best friend, David Fox, who patiently listened to my reading of each revision. (That's what you get for marrying a writer!) Our walking conversations about trust, identity, opinions, assumptions, beliefs, and self-confidence have found their way from our neighborhood to these pages.

Contents

Introduction

Hi. I'm an online advisor at a Web site for teens (www.theinsite.org). Many visitors of the site email me questions about what's going on in their lives. Middle school issues come up a lot, so I thought, "Hey, why not write a book about this?"

Middle school can be cool but also stressful. Maybe you have a packed schedule and more homework than ever. Friendships may be shifting, and things at home might also be changing. Other people's opinions can start to seem very important—especially their opinion of you. If you compare yourself to others and don't believe you measure up in looks, smarts, athletic ability, or popularity, you might wonder if there's something wrong with you.

It's normal to want to fit in, and lots of people feel pressure to go along with everyone else or do whatever it takes to avoid getting picked on. If this sounds familiar, this book may be able to help. It's all about being who you want to be and feeling good about that. Confidence gives you power. If other people try to bring you down or push you around, you can use that power to keep it together and figure out your next move.

Throughout the book you'll find the stories of six teens trying to figure out middle school, quotes and advice from real teens, quizzes, tips, and insider tools for staying strong through the rough spots. As you read, I hope you'll feel free to email me (help4kids@freespirit.com) with any thoughts, questions, or stories of your own.

In friendship,
Annie

We go to Milldale Middle School.

We're very different in lots of ways, but we're all good friends. A couple months ago, we were just hanging out when these kids came over....

Just so you know, we're normal teens. We don't like everybody and we don't expect everyone to like us. Our school is probably like yours. There are plenty of nice people and some bullies, too. If by some miracle the bullies got an attitude transplant and the teasing stopped, everyone in Milldale (including us) would be happier. We'd be friends with the people we're friends with. And the other kids would leave us alone.

Anyway, after those guys left, Mateo said he was fed up with being teased because of his height. Abby totally understood because people always call her names like "lard butt." The rest of us don't get picked on because of our looks, but we still have plenty of things we'd like to change about ourselves. Chris hates that he's got ADD. Michelle wishes that she stressed less about grades. Jen admits that she worries a lot about what other people think. Jack doesn't like talking about feelings so it's hard to know what he thinks, but he did say he wanted to beat up those guys for making fun of Mateo.

As we were talking, Michelle, who's really smart, came up with one of her probing questions:

How about that? We always thought the problem was the mean kids giving us a hard time. Turns out we're not always so nice to ourselves. There's that voice inside our head saying things like: **"I'm not smart enough ... Not strong enough ... Not hot enough ... Not cool enough ... Not good enough!"** Maybe you've heard it, too.

When we criticize ourselves it brings us down, but we don't know how to stop. It's like we're in this race. Nobody actually entered, but everyone's in it and we all want to win. So we try to be like the kids everyone likes so people will like us, too. We watch what we do and say so we don't make mistakes and embarrass ourselves. We hate being in the race, but that's the way it is in middle school and there's nothing we can do about it.

Or is there?

We hear that things get easier in high school. We don't know if that's true, but thinking about it gives us hope. It also gave Michelle an idea: "Why don't we ask other kids how they deal with these problems?"

Turns out lots of kids had great advice about getting through middle school—secret information that no one tells you about. **That's why this series is called "Middle School Confidential"—because not everyone knows the things we've found out.** Like, how to quit worrying about what other people think. That advice really helped us.

Jen

Jack

Not that we've totally stopped worrying . . . we still do. But little by little, we've started caring less about what "they" think and started having more fun just **BEING OURSELVES.**

"MY BIGGEST PROBLEM IN LIFE IS MY WEIGHT! EVERYONE IS ALWAYS TEASING ME! AT HOME, AT SCHOOL . . . EVEN PEOPLE I DON'T KNOW! IT REALLY GETS ME DOWN."
— ANTHONY, 13

I KNOW HOW THIS GUY FEELS!

WHEN PEOPLE CALL ME EL SHRIMPO I'M IN A BAD MOOD FOR THE REST OF THE DAY.

DON'T LET IT GET TO YOU, MAT.

When you're in a good mood you might look in the mirror and think, "I look good!" That probably makes you feel more confident.

But if you have a look when you're angry, sad, or worried, you may not like what you see. You might even make rude comments to yourself. Or other people may tease you. That can make you feel insecure and change the way you feel about yourself and the way you act.

When you feel down about your looks, what's really going on? Do you suddenly look different? Not likely. But maybe your mood is making it hard for you to see yourself the way you really are. Maybe you are just comparing yourself to some "perfect" person and don't feel like you measure up. Or maybe you're starting to believe what the teasers are saying.

The truth is, nobody is "perfect." Pro athletes may be bulked up on steroids. Supermodels' photos are often touched up by computers. **And people who tease you have their own problems— that's why they're taking things out on YOU.**

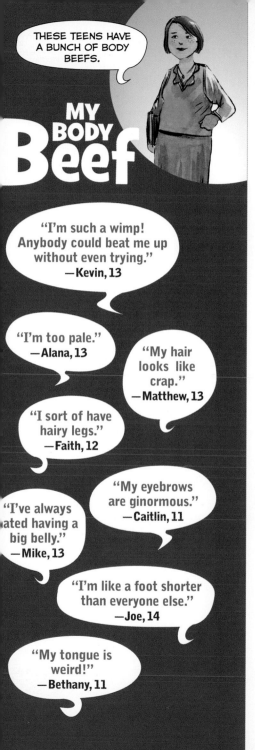

THESE TEENS HAVE A BUNCH OF BODY BEEFS.

MY BODY Beef

"I'm such a wimp! Anybody could beat me up without even trying."
—Kevin, 13

"I'm too pale."
—Alana, 13

"My hair looks like crap."
—Matthew, 13

"I sort of have hairy legs."
—Faith, 12

"My eyebrows are ginormous."
—Caitlin, 11

"I've always hated having a big belly."
—Mike, 13

"I'm like a foot shorter than everyone else."
—Joe, 14

"My tongue is weird!"
—Bethany, 11

ADS MESS WITH YOUR MIND

Slick ads and hi-tech marketing messages are designed to manipulate the way you think. Teens spend billions each year buying certain sodas, snacks, fast food, hair products, makeup, designer clothes, and tech toys because they think: "If I buy this, I'll be cool!" You don't need to buy anything to make you a better person. And you don't need to let the media define you or mess with your confidence.

Companies don't want to waste their advertising dollars. That's why they always know exactly who they want to target with their ads. How can you be a smart media consumer? By opening your mind and paying attention to media messages. Next time you see a TV commercial or an ad online or in a magazine, ask yourself:

- **Who is this ad aimed at?**

- **What's the message here?**

- **What do I think when I see the ad?**

- **How does it make me feel about the product?**

- **How does it make me feel about myself?**

Sometimes people say things without meaning to hurt anyone, but feelings get hurt anyway. Everyone's made mistakes like that. That's when a simple apology can make everyone involved feel much better. But sometimes people say things because they're trying to hurt someone. **USING WORDS AS WEAPONS IS A FORM OF VIOLENCE.** Maybe you never thought about it that way, but it's true. **If you've ever been teased, you probably also know that some insults have a way of staying with you, even after the teasing stops.**

From the "I Get Teased" Files

"There's a group of boys that teases me about my small bottom. It embarrasses me and makes me feel out of place."
—Anya, 13

"People say that I get mad too easily. Sometimes they egg me on to make me lose my temper."
—Lawrence, 14

"I'm very tall for my age, but I still weigh too much. Some of the other kids put me down."
—Rashard, 13

"People make fun of me by calling me names like 'pig,' 'gorilla,' and 'uni-brow.' It makes me feel really bad."
—Addison, 12

"At my old school I was bullied. Now my best guy friend at my new school doesn't understand why I'm so sensitive."
—Rosie, 11

DEALING WITH TEASING

Teasing and bullying are common challenges for many students. And the problem is at its worst in middle school. While you can't control what other people do, think, or say, you do have choices when it comes to how you'll respond. Here are five things to keep in mind when dealing with bullying and teasing:

1. This isn't your fault. You haven't done anything to deserve harassment.

2. Responding to bullying with violence, put-downs, or threats of your own can only make a situation worse. If you choose not to play the game the bully is playing, you'll keep your self-respect and be much better off.

3. Don't believe what others say. It's bad enough when people put you down, but when you replay their rude comments over in your mind, you hurt yourself again and again.

4. Change your response to the teasing. When you choose to let someone make you feel bad, you give them power. Let the teasing roll off and you take back that power. It's not easy to block out put-downs or gossip, but you can try. When others are being mean to you, for example, do your best to remember all of the great qualities you have.

5. Don't suffer in silence. Tell adults at home about the bullying. Together you can let school staff know what's happening and make sure they do something about it. If you're not comfortable talking to your family about the problem, discuss it with another trusted adult. When you speak up for yourself, things can change for the better.

YOUR BODY IS PROBABLY STILL GROWING.
THAT EXPLAINS WHY YOU MAY BE HUNGRY ALL THE TIME.

Eating junk food once in a while isn't going to hurt you, but overdoing it will fill you up and out—without giving your body the nutrients it needs. On the other hand, eating healthy (while also getting the exercise and rest you need) can make you feel stronger and more confident all around.

It's true that finding time to eat well can be difficult. Some days you may have to grab meals on the run, and the quickest option might be a burger and fries at a fast food place. Finding healthy snacks can also be a challenge—if candy and chips are all that's available, that's probably what you'll eat. Planning ahead can help. If you know you'll have trouble finding healthy foods, pack your own lunch with enough healthy snacks to give you energy throughout the day wherever you are.

Another issue that can make healthy eating a challenge: Most teens don't buy food for the family. Even if you decide to eat better, you may have to convince your parents to make some changes. If this is true in your home, go ahead and make your best case for healthier food options. Explain why you'd like to eat less junk and more fresh fruit, veggies, salads, lean meats, nuts, whole grains, and other foods that are good for you. If everyone gets healthier, they'll be thanking you!

THESE KIDS CHANGED THEIR ATTITUDES ABOUT THEIR LOOKS.

I'm OKAY with the way I am ...

"You think every flaw on your body is marked with flashing lights. (It isn't!) I ask myself: 'Do people really notice that?' Even if they do they probably really don't care!"
— Petra, 14

"Whatever hurtful things people say to me are probably just a reflection of their own insecurities. I ignore them or laugh to show people that it doesn't bother me."
— Peter, 13

"Because I'm short, other kids have laughed at me and said I look like an elf. I used to get offended, but then I told them that I like myself and I couldn't care less what they say about me. They stopped making fun of me."
— John, 12

"Sometimes I see other girls and wish I looked like them. But, like my mom said, they might wish the same thing when they see me."
— Amber, 13

Not okay with who you are? Get help!

Blubberbuster.com
www.blubberbuster.com
This site is all about helping overweight teens take charge of their health. You'll find support for healthy weight loss, success stories, and interesting food facts. (For example, to work off a double-scoop ice-cream cone you'd have to run 10 miles!)

National Eating Disorders Association
www.nationaleatingdisorders.org
If you or a friend has gone from wanting to get in shape to extreme dieting and over-exercising, then what started out as a healthy choice may now be an eating disorder. This site has answers and advice about anorexia, bulimia, and binge eating.

Boys Town National Hotline
1-800-448-3000
Not feeling good about how you look or who you are is serious. Many teens with body image and confidence issues hurt themselves by cutting or attempting suicide. If you feel like you want to hurt yourself, it's important to talk with someone right away. The Boys Town National Hotline (for boys and girls) is a 24-hour helpline you can turn to if you feel like you don't have anyone to talk to.

Everyone enjoys hearing that people like them and that they look good. But if you don't believe the compliments deep inside, then what other people say isn't going to boost your ego much. Real confidence starts with you liking *you*. When you have that piece of the puzzle, then what other people say (good, bad, or in between) doesn't matter as much. If you do want to make improvements to your body, change what you can change and change your attitude about the rest.

No matter what you look like, a positive attitude about yourself is your secret weapon. Respect yourself in what you do, what you say, and the way you think, and you'll build your self-confidence from the inside out.

My Plate
www.myplate.gov
It doesn't help to sit around wishing for a different body. Eating healthy is one way to get serious about the shape you're in and take charge of your health. You can check out this site for insider information on a menu that's just right for you.

President's Council on Sports, Fitness, & Nutrition
www.health.gov/our-work/pcsfn
Getting in shape means getting active. You'll burn fat, add muscle, and feel better. This site has tools you can use to get started on an exercise program. A word of advice: Pick an activity or a sport you like and you're much more likely to stick with your routine.

TeensHealth
www.teenshealth.org
Your mind is as much a part of you as your body, and negative thinking can hurt your health in serious ways. This site has information you can use to stay healthy in mind, body, and spirit.

Chapter 2: Sometimes I Worry What Other People Think

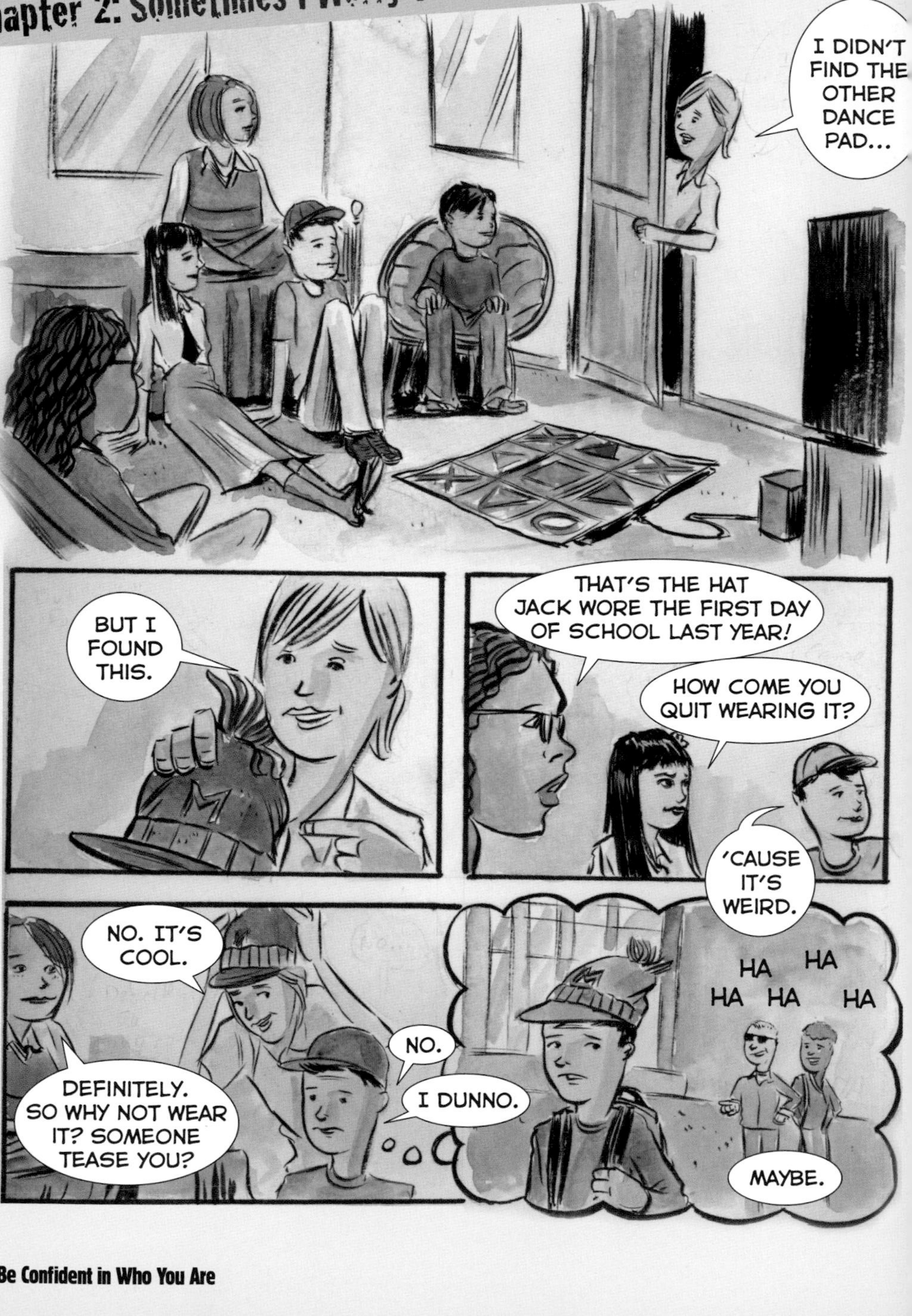

IT'S SO UNFAIR! PEOPLE SHOULD BE ABLE TO WEAR WHAT THEY WANT!

AND LOOK THE WAY THEY LOOK WITHOUT GETTING TEASED!

PROBING QUESTION! WHY DOES WHAT THEY THINK MATTER SO MUCH TO US?

'CAUSE WE WANT TO FIT IN.

AND BE LIKED.

AND RESPECTED.

I'M JUST TRYING TO BE LESS OF AN OUTCAST THAN I ALREADY AM!

HA! HA! HA! HA! HA! HA! HA!

I JUST DO WHATEVER THE POPULAR PEOPLE DO, THEN I KNOW I'LL BE LIKED.

Pretty much everybody worries a little about what other people think. Even teens who say they don't worry about other people's opinions, probably do ... at least sometimes.

If humans were like some reptiles, we'd be complete loners. We wouldn't think about other reptiles—except maybe to eat them! But people live in groups and we need to get along to survive. That's why everyone wants to be liked and accepted. It's human nature. There's only a problem when worrying about what others think gets in the way of being yourself.

Wondering if what you're doing is okay with the people around you makes it hard to relax. If you spend lots of time trying to be someone you're not—or trying to be invisible so people won't make fun of you—how can you feel confident and happy?

Why I Care What OTHER People Think

"I don't want to lose my popular status."
—Gabriella, 13

"It's annoying when people make fun of you."
—Bryant, 11

"Society is not exactly nice about the way you look or act if it doesn't fit into the bubble of 'what's cool.'"
—Eric, 14

"If the popular people don't like you then you are most likely seen as a loser or an outcast."
—Stephen, 13

"I tried hard to fit in with all the preps and they were nothing but mean to me. Even then I still wanted them to like me."
—Maria, 13

"People are always talking about what they like and don't like in others. I feel like I'm forced to do what everyone else is doing so I don't feel left out."
—Rose, 12

WHAT I LIKE ABOUT MYSELF

You can't please everyone all the time, so why try? **Be pleased with yourself and you'll always have at least one person on your side. Focusing on your strengths is one way to remember all of the great things that you have going for you. Not sure what your good qualities are? Ask yourself:**

1. What am I good at doing?
2. What do I like about my personality?
3. In what ways do I show that I'm a good and interesting person?

Make a list of the things you respect and admire about yourself. After you're done, think of how you can do a better job of showing people who you really are—without bragging or bringing others down.

Drawing the line means knowing what's right for you, and sticking to it, no matter what other people say. That usually works out in familiar settings where right and wrong are pretty obvious. But because middle school presents a lot of new situations, you may find yourself in unexplored territory. If something has never happened to you before, how can you know the right thing to do? You can't. Not instantly. Not always.

You are the only one who knows what's right for you, but sometimes it's hard to trust what you know. Suppose you've always told yourself that you'll never smoke. Then someone you want to be friends with asks you to smoke with him. If you refuse, he might make fun of you. If you cross the line and smoke, things can get very complicated. You may have to hide the cigarette smell on your clothes and your breath or lie to your parents and nonsmoking friends. You may become addicted and have real difficulty giving it up. On top of all that, you'll probably lose some self-respect for going back on your word.

So even though you can't always know what to do, it can help to think about what's right for you—and what might happen if you . . .

. . . CROSS THE LINE.

HERE'S WHERE
I DRAW THE LINE ...

"No drugs or alcohol. Some of my friends have done it, and man are they screwed up now!"
—Thomas, 14

"I hate people pressuring me to do things I don't want to do. If I say no it's no, that's the end of it."
—Nick, 13

"I'd never lie or break a promise."
—Moni, 11

"When people are gossiping about my friends I can't stand it. Especially when people don't even know what they're talking about."
—Alex, 13

"Verbal abuse is something that I take very seriously. I've had friends suffer from it and it changed them. It infuriates me how teachers, parents, and counselors don't take it seriously enough."
—Marcus, 13

"It's stupid to starve yourself just to be thin. You don't have to be skinny to be beautiful."
—Callie, 12

"If I have a boyfriend who pushes me to go further than I want to, I have to break up with him—even if I like him a lot."
—Angela, 14

Need to Know?

Above the Influence
www.abovetheinfluence.com

It isn't always easy to disagree with your friends. Sometimes it takes a lot of courage to say, "You guys go ahead without me." You may feel left out or lonely, but you'll have your self-respect—and other people will often respect you more, too. This Web site has a lot of smart strategies for dealing with peer pressure.

The Girls by Amy Goldman Koss. The six girls in this tight middle school clique each have a lot to say about who's in and who's out. As they get real with themselves and each other, they get closer to figuring out what matters even more than popularity.

The Misfits by James Howe. When an unlikely group of friends reaches middle school, the other students give them a really hard time. In response, the friends decide to run for student council against the more popular kids.

Trino's Choice by Diane Gonzales Bertrand. Trino's family life is far from great, so when a gang member offers him an opportunity to make some "easy money," Trino is tempted. But his crush on a very different kind of girl provides him with another choice.

People will always have their own opinions.

You'll agree with some and not with others. But other people's opinions only matter as much as you let them. If you worry too much about what others think, you might be missing out on new experiences. Be honest: Have you ever held yourself back from doing something because you were afraid you might be made fun of?

The truth is that doing your own thing—whether it's sitting with new people at lunch or trying something you've never done before—can make you more confident in who you are.

If I didn't have to worry about what other people think . . .

CHECK OUT WHAT THESE TEENS SAID!

"It would be much easier for me to talk to people because I wouldn't have to act cooler than the person I was talking to. I think that might actually make me cooler."
—Eduardo 13

"The first thing I'd do is try out for football with the boys."
—Lisette, 12

"I'd definitely stop spending a lot of money on stupid things just to fit in."
—Casey, 14

"I wouldn't need to formulate the perfect words to say to those perfect people. Instead I would say exactly how I feel."
—Antoinette, 13

"For sure I'd stop lying to impress people."
—Cassandra, 12

"Little kids always have a great day because they never even notice what other people are wearing, saying about them, or what their reputation is. Instead they are always trying to have fun and be themselves. I'd like to be like that again."
—Kevin, 11

"Not worrying what people think of you means you are un-insultable. If what they say is true, I already know it. If what they say is false, then how can it insult me?"
—Byron, 14

"I wouldn't be self-conscious 24/7. Instead I would go through life as happily as possible—that's the point of living here on Earth, right?"
—Erika, 13

Do I worry TOO MUCH
about what other people think?

1. If other people think something is funny, I laugh even if I don't agree.
T or F

2. If everyone has seen a movie that I haven't seen, I'll say I saw it.
T or F

3. I hardly ever tell people how I really feel.
T or F

4. I try really hard not to make a fool of myself.
T or F

5. I wish I could read people's minds.
T or F

6. I've dropped out of an activity because none of my friends were into it.
T or F

7. I stress if I think people are talking about me.
T or F

8. If someone makes fun of what I'm wearing, I won't wear it again.
T or F

9. If my friends hate a TV show that I like, I'll pretend I hate it.
T or F

10. I'm never the first person to give my opinion.
T or F

Answers:

7–10 Trues: You worry what other people think and it brings you down. With a boost in self-confidence and support from friends, you will trust yourself more and enjoy being you.

3–6 Trues: Sometimes it's hard for you to stand up for yourself, but when you do, it feels good. You're getting better all the time at being your own person.

0–2 Trues: You hardly ever worry what others think because you're self-confident and have lots of self-respect. You may not know it, but people respect you for who you are.

MENTAL MOVIES

Daydreaming can be fun when you choose to do it. But when you're worried about other people's opinions, you may suddenly be stuck watching a mental movie rated "S" (for Stress). If people are pressuring you, your mental movies about what might happen can make you feel tense and unsure of yourself. They can also lower your self-confidence. Even though mental movies might seem real, they're just thoughts and they do not predict the future.

Here's how to get yourself unplugged from any mental movie that brings you down:

1. Try to catch yourself watching a mental movie. It's tricky, but you can do it. One clue is that feeling of "spacing out."

2. Now, stop and take some slow, even, deep breaths. Breathe in and think, "I am now breathing in." Breathe out and think, "I am now breathing out." This can help get you out of your thoughts and bring you back to right here and now.

3. Look around you and focus on something you've never noticed before. Appreciate what you see. Smile.

Getting back in control of your mental movies can help you de-stress and feel better about yourself.

It's not always easy to trust that you know what's right for you. Especially when some people might be telling you not to trust yourself but to trust them instead. Question what people tell you, and then think for yourself. Nobody knows you better than you do. When you keep that in mind you probably make your best decisions—the ones that reflect who you really are.

WHATCHA DOIN'?

OOH, SOKO!

IT'S CALLED SUDOKU.

MAYBE IT'S 6.

LOOKS IMPOSSIBLE. YOU DOING IT FOR EXTRA CREDIT?

BZZZZ

8?

6?

BZZZZ

IT'S 7! NO! THAT'S WRONG!

BZZZZ

JUST FOR FUN.

Have you ever lost control so that you said or did something you regretted? The truth is we all have—whether we want to admit it or not.

Staying calm, cool, and in charge of your behavior can be tricky, especially when there are plenty of situations that can push your "out-of-control" button—ex-best friends talking (or texting) about you behind your back, being bullied, parents or teachers who seem to treat you unfairly, to name just a few. What do you normally do when things like that happen? Out-stab the backstabbers? Bully back? Mouth off to adults?

It can be tempting to get back at others in tense moments, and the brain can actually make it hard to do anything else. How? Certain key areas, like those in charge of impulse control and weighing consequences, aren't fully developed until age 22 or later. So when something or someone pushes your buttons, strong feelings like anger or frustration can easily hijack your brain so that you lash out in a rage or do something else without thinking.

Knowing what's going on in your brain can help you understand why it's tough to stay in control. But tough or not, it's important not to let your actions hurt others—or yourself.

You've got a right to feel whatever you're feeling, but you don't have the right to express those feelings in any way you want.

I GUESS I'M NOT THE ONLY ONE WHO LOSES IT.

...rom the
I lost it ..."
-ILES

"I threw a controller at the TV because I lost a game. It was totally destroyed."
—Charlie, 14

"My mom wouldn't let me go out with my friends so I punched a wall in my basement and my knuckles started to bleed."
—Adonis, 12

"One day when I was under a lot of pressure I screamed at my friend for no reason and made her cry."
—Tori, 11

"This girl at my old school was teasing my friend so I slapped her."
—Cherise, 13

"My friend was being kinda annoying so I told him to leave me alone and never talk to me again. He took me very seriously and we're no longer friends."
— Rafael, 13

"I said something terrible to my sister and trashed her room."
—Ivana, 13

6 Tips for Staying Cool

1. **Know your buttons.** If you've figured out that certain situations bother you, avoid them as often as possible.

2. **Recognize when you're about to lose control.** Do you have racing thoughts? Does your heart beat faster? Knowing what usually happens inside you right before you lose it can help you stay in control.

3. **Stop.** It's not easy to stop a runaway train, but sometimes that's what you need to do. If you feel like you're losing it, don't wait. Hit the brakes!

4. **Give yourself some space.** Just getting out of a stressful situation can really help you calm down. Take a walk or get some air if you feel ready to explode.

5. **Breathe.** Breathe in, slowly, through your nose. Breathe out, slowly, through your open mouth. Repeat 5–10 times. You'll lower your heart rate and quiet your mind so you can think more clearly.

6. **Talk to someone.** There's no need to figure everything out on your own. Support from someone you trust can help you get back in control so you can figure out what to do next.

No one should expect you to be perfect.

(Hopefully you don't expect that of yourself either.)

You're probably going to make some mistakes—like arguing with adults at home when you don't like their rules or copping a negative attitude when your coach doesn't give you enough playing time. When you realize what you've done, say you're sorry. Apologizing when you need to can help you strengthen friendships, keep the peace with adults, and be more understanding and forgiving when someone hurts your feelings.

If you don't know exactly what to say after you've lost it, writing about it or talking to someone you trust can help. When you're ready to apologize, what you say isn't as important as how you say it. Be sincere. When you mean what you say and honestly try not to make the same mistake again, things will probably get better.

I'M SORRY . . .

"I hope my friends can forgive me for getting caught up in being popular and pretending I didn't know them. They were always the best friends ever and I am sorry."
—Wanda, 12

"I told my cousin I wished she was dead. After that, she got cancer and I blamed myself. Thankfully, she is healthy again. I have apologized to her, but I hope she knows how truly sorry I am."
—Margarita, 11

"I'd like to apologize to my English teacher for giving him the finger."
—Shawn, 14

"My dad has always been there for me, yet I still don't appreciate him. He's the only person I let my anger out on, but I really don't mean to."
—Frannie, 12

"I have been pressuring my friends to tell m other people's secrets. I want to say I'm sor and that they should please tell me to stop i start doing it again without realizing it."
—Li, 12

"I am totally rude to my mom sometimes, a she is the one who brought me into this world should be more grateful and respectful to her
—Zoe, 13

"I'd like to think that all the good things I do my relationship with my girlfriend outweigh t. stupid stuff. But every now and then, the tru hits me in the chest like a battering ram, and realize that I'm very selfish. I'd like to apologi: to her for not being a better boyfriend."
—Domingo, 14

"I'm always a pain in the butt to my sibling I'd like to apologize to them."
—Thomas, 13

MAKING THE PEACE

Do you need another good reason to apologize?
Even if you believe the other person was wrong, there may be a part of you that doesn't feel great about the way you handled things. Making the peace with another person can also help you make things right with yourself. It's not so hard to do:

1. Take a break. If you've lost control you may need some time to calm down.

2. Investigate. Sometimes anger may be covering up hurt, frustration, or fear. Instead of admitting how you really feel, you may get angry at yourself or at someone else. It might even be someone who has nothing to do with it! Try to figure out what was really going on right before you lost your temper.

3. Question. Ask yourself: "What did I do th added to the problem?" "What could I differently next time?"

4. Question again. When you were feeling ove whelmed, you probably weren't communicati very well. Now that you're calmer, ask yourse "What do I really want to say?"

5. Apologize. If you hurt someone, say you're sor Tell the truth about what was actually going with you.

6. Plan for the future. Make an agreement th the next time something like this comes up, y will try to control yourself and talk about ho you're feeling.

Am I the Boss of My ANGER?

QUIZ

1. You're next in line at the food counter when someone cuts in front. You:
   a) shove the guy and tell him to get to the back of the line.
   b) don't say anything and think, "Why do people always do this to me?"
   c) calmly explain that you were there first.
   d) mutter something rude under your breath.

2. Your sister accidentally spills juice on your homework. You:
   a) scream and call her names.
   b) close your eyes and think, "I am doomed."
   c) grab your homework and ask her to get some paper towels.
   d) storm out of the room and mess up something of hers.

3. You're running late for class and trying to get your math book from your locker, but you can't remember the combination. You:
   a) kick the locker and curse.
   b) start crying and wonder, "Why am I such a loser?"
   c) take some slow deep breaths and calm down so you can remember your combination.
   d) get to class late and lie about why you don't have your book.

4. You and a friend are at her apartment planning to do something when her phone rings. You overhear her say: "I'm not doing anything. [Your name] is here, but she's just leaving. I'll be over in 20 minutes." When your friend hangs up, you:
   a) storm out of the apartment.
   b) pretend you didn't hear anything and wonder why nobody likes you.
   c) tell your friend how you feel and wait to hear what she has to say.
   d) make up an excuse and leave. On the way home, you imagine ways to get back at your friend.

5. You're studying for a test. Your parents turn on the TV really loud. You:
   a) burst into the room yelling, "Turn that down!"
   b) struggle to study and think, "Nobody in this family cares about me."
   c) tell your parents, "I'm trying to study. Could you please turn it down?"
   d) get angrier and blast your music just to annoy them.

If you got:

Mostly A's: When you get angry you may feel out of control. You might say and do things that leave other people feeling hurt. To avoid these problems, try to calm down and think before you act.

Mostly B's: When you get angry it may be hard for you to say how you really feel. You may also believe that people are against you. To do a better job of standing up for yourself, practice telling "safe" people (like family members) what you want and need.

Mostly C's: When you get angry you know how to control your behavior so no one gets hurt. You also know how to take care of yourself by telling people how you feel without being disrespectful.

Mostly D's: When you get angry you sometimes bottle up the feelings inside and can end up lying or trying to get revenge on people. That's not healthy and it's not the best way to stand up for yourself and be responsible. Feelings are easier to manage if you express them as they come up.

When it's time to GET HELP . . .

It's important to talk with someone you trust ASAP if you are:

- physically hurting yourself or someone else.
- frequently overwhelmed by feelings of sadness, hopelessness, or anger.
- using alcohol or other drugs.
- feeling out of control or abused in a relationship.
- worried or scared about something going on at home.

If you're not comfortable talking with a parent, school counselor, or any other adult in your life, you can call the **Boys Town National Hotline (1-800-448-3000)**—a 24/7 helpline for teens.

Sure, you're going to be in a bad mood once in a while. That's normal. But pretty much everyone agrees that it's more fun (for you and the people around you) to be in a good mood. Doing things you enjoy can help you be happier. The same goes for taking good care of your body. Try these tips and see if they help you feel calmer and more balanced.

1. Exercise. Engaging in sports, dance, martial arts, or other physical activities is great for your body, your mood, and your mind.

2. Eat healthy. Good food is also good news for your body and mood. Research suggests that some foods—like green, orange, and yellow veggies—can be especially helpful in lowering stress.

3. Sleep. A good night's rest will put you in a better position to deal with whatever comes your way. Doctors recommend that teens get at least nine and a half hours of sleep each night.

4. Hang out with friends and family. Spend time with people you like and who accept you. They are your support network, and just being with them is good for you.

5. Take a break every day. At least once a day, take a break and relax—walk the dog, play with the cat, read for enjoyment, play a game, take a bath, write in a journal, listen to or play music. Doing the things you like to do (not just those you have to do) helps keep you centered.

No one can stay completely in control of strong feelings like anger all of the time, but that's not the goal. Instead, it's figuring out your best move at the moment you're feeling short-tempered—whether that's walking away, finding someone you can talk to, or another way to calm down. **If you slip up and make a mistake, take responsibility for what's happened by apologizing to anyone you've hurt.** At the same time, try to learn something that will make it easier for you to do the right thing next time.

Mad: How to Deal with Your Anger and Get Respect by James J. Crist. Anger is a normal human emotion, and no one should be ashamed of feeling it. The key is to deal with strong feelings in positive ways. This book provides practical strategies for staying cool and making good decisions when tempers threaten to flare.

Teens Health
www.teenshealth.org
Losing control gets attention, but it rarely gets you what you need. This site offers information to help you stay in control and make choices that will help a situation—not make it worse.

Chapter 4: Meet the Opinionator

"I GET JEALOUS OF OTHER PEOPLE BECAUSE I ALWAYS HAVE IN THE BACK OF MY MIND HOW EVERYONE IS BETTER THAN ME. HOW CAN I CHANGE MY THINKING IN ORDER TO INCREASE MY SELF-CONFIDENCE AND NOT BE SO JEALOUS?"
— APRIL, 13

ALL THAT "IN THE BACK OF THE MIND" STUFF COMES FROM THE OPINIONATOR.

WHO'S THE OPINIONATOR? SOME SUPERHERO?

NAH! THE OPINIONATOR WHAT I CALL THE VOICE INSIDE MY HEAD.

THAT GUY'S WAY BETTER THAN ME! HIS SKATEBOARD'S COOLER THAN MINE! THIS SHIRT MAKES ME LOOK LIKE AN IDIOT!

Opinion-ator

school
friends
food
girls
family

IT'S ALWAYS TELLING ME WHEN SOMEONE OR SOMETHING IS NOT GOOD ENOUGH.

NOT GOOD ENOUGH TO DO WHAT?

TO MAKE THIS JUMP.

MY OPINIONATOR SAYS IT AND I BELIEVE IT. SHAKES MY CONFIDENCE. WATCH!

YOU ALL RIGHT, CHRIS?

YEAH, BUT SEE? I'M A LOUSY SKATER.

MY OPINIONATOR SAYS I'M TOO SHORT.

AW, MATEO, YOU'RE A CUTIE. AND THAT'S A FACT!

NO, JEN, A FACT IS SOMETHING YOU CAN PROVE. WHETHER SOMEONE'S "CUTE" IS YOUR OPINION.

You probably know that the little voice inside your head isn't always your friend. Why not? **Because it can make you doubt yourself.** In fact, sometimes it's great at that. Picture this, you're watching TV or talking to a friend, just trying to live your life, when a random thought pops in, "I'll never be able to do that." "Everyone has a girlfriend but me!" "Her life is so much better than mine." That kind of thinking can eat away at your confidence, making it hard for you to be happy with yourself.

These thoughts, coming straight from your Opinionator, bully you from inside your brain. And even if you know, deep down, that they are just thoughts, not rules—and for sure, not facts—it can still be very hard to ignore them.

CHECK OUT WHAT THEIR OPINIONATORS SAY.

The OPINIONATOR Says ...

"I am just a mess when it comes to relationships."
—Marcia, 13

"It's like I'm too young for everything."
—Jorges, 11

"I'm stuck in a dead end."
—Pamela, 14

"I'm afraid to stick up for myself."
—Wang, 13

"I should learn to act my age."
—Nikki, 13

"Sometimes I feel like I'm just too stupid to understand the work at school."
—Zack, 12

"Since my mom remarried I feel like I'm just a nuisance to her."
—Nicholas, 12

FACTS ABOUT OPINIONS

Opinions are personal points of view, but a fact is true and can be proved. You find opinions on the Internet; in newspapers, books, and magazines; and coming out of people's mouths all the time. Here are some facts about opinions:

- **Some opinions are meant to hurt you, confuse you, or put you down. ("You're such a pathetic loser.")**
- **Some opinions are meant to persuade you. ("Buy this product. It's the best.")**
- **Some opinions are meant to help you make healthier choices. ("You need to calm down.")**

When you hear an opinion from someone, think for yourself and answer these questions about it:

1. Is this opinion meant to hurt me or help me?

2. Does it match what I know to be true as a fact?

3. People may try to get you to do things based on their opinions. Before you go ahead, ask yourself, "Is this the right thing to do?"

If you answer "no" to number 3, you know it's time to draw the line. If you're not sure, then ask for a second opinion from someone you trust. Listen to this person's advice and think again about what's right for you.

FACT OR OPINION? QUIZ

1. Whoa, dude! You need a shower. **F or O**
2. He doesn't know what he's talking about. **F or O**
3. That was the best movie ever. **F or O**
4. That's a really lame joke. **F or O**
5. Her reasons for being mad are stupid. **F or O**
6. I'm such an idiot. **F or O**
7. That shirt is weird. **F or O**
8. I have the world's smartest dog. **F or O**
9. Cool shoes! **F or O**
10. She's prettier than me. **F or O**
11. Earth has one moon. **F or O**
12. That music stinks. **F or O**
13. Dolphins are mammals. **F or O**
14. You're awesome! **F or O**
15. He got the highest score on the test. **F or O**

Answers:

1. **F** (If it's after P.E. it's probably a fact! Otherwise, it may be an opinion.)
2. **O** (Unless he tells you he doesn't know what he's talking about.)
3. **O** (Even if you and a million other people agree.)
4. **O** (What people think of a joke, a movie, a song, is their opinion.)
5. **O** (If you spread it around, her opinion of you will not be good.)
6. **O** (The average IQ is 91–110. You may not always make "smart" choices, but unless your IQ is less than 20, you are not an "idiot.")
7. **O** (What looks cool in fashion and appearance is all about opinion.)
8. **O** (Of course your dog is truly great, but "smartest in the world" is impossible to prove, so, it's an opinion.)
9. **O** (See #7)
10. **O** (The definition of "pretty" is an opinion.)
11. **F** (We've all seen it and a few people have even been there.)
12. **O** (See #4)
13. **F** (They're also incredible, but that's an opinion.)
14. **O** (But always great to hear.)
15. **F** (The numbers prove it.)

IF HER OPINIONATOR SAYS SHE'S TOO TALKATIVE SHOULDN'T SHE LISTEN?

SURE!

DUST!

ESPECIALLY IF SHE'S BEING REALLY ANNOYING!

HA!

HA!

HA!

HA!

HA!

HA!

HA!

WHAT'S THE DIFFERENCE BETWEEN CONSTRUCTIVE CRITICISM AND A PUT-DOWN?

WHEN SOMEONE TELLS YOU SOMETHING THAT YOU REALLY NEED TO CHANGE, MY UNCLE CALLS IT CONSTRUCTIVE CRITICISM.

MAYBE IT'S THE WAY YOU FEEL WHEN YOU HEAR IT.

A put-down is meant to hurt or embarrass you.
That's never going to feel good. But constructive criticism is meant to help you.

So what about the "talkative" girl? Is she putting herself down or giving herself constructive criticism? It's impossible to tell without knowing her, but let's say she isn't any more talkative than her friends. What if this all started with someone's Opinionator? If the girl lost her confidence and decided not to talk anymore, that sure could hold her back and make her unhappy.

Your Opinionator will probably never shut up completely—neither will anyone else's for that matter. But that's okay. You might just need to figure out when to listen and when not to bother. If your Opinionator broadcasts thoughts that cheer you up and build you up, turn up the volume.

But if what you're hearing are put-downs, tune it out, because no one should be messing with your self-confidence—especially not you.

How to be more self-confident

"I surround myself with people who don't make me doubt myself."
—LeeAnn, 14

"I try new things, even if I'm uncertain how things will turn out. It's worth it because I use that to build confidence."
—Simon, 14

"I practice talking to others with people I'm never going to see again. It helps me express myself better and raises my self-esteem."
—Angelo, 13

"I do the things I do well—like writing. I feel like I am more special."
—Jesse, 13

"After I've had a run or played tennis, I feel so alive—like I can do anything! When I'm positive it affects other people, too, and makes them happy as well."
—Debbi, 12

"Why would I want to be sad all the time when I can choose to stay a kid at heart and not grow up too soon?"
—Rob, 11

"I'm realistic. I know I'm not going to be liked by everybody, but I try to be the best person I can be and keep the faith that I will have my day."
—Tyrone, 12

Give Yourself a
CONFIDENCE
BOOST

Next time you're low on self-confidence and your Opinionator is filling your head with negative thoughts, try this:

1. **Ask, "What am I really feeling right now and why?"**
   Maybe it's, "I'm worried about the game." Or, "I'm scared to talk to my crush." Whatever it is, tell yourself the truth.

2. **Breathe deeply.**
   Take some slow deep breaths and calm down.

3. **Give yourself a pep talk.**
   You might say, "I can do this" or "I'm going to give it my best shot."

4. **Create a game plan.**
   Knowing exactly how you're going to get something done adds to your confidence going in. So make a list of action steps.

5. **Go ahead.**
   Do what you need to do.

6. **Nice going!**
   When you've finished the task, congratulate yourself. You deserve it.

If you're not comfortable going ahead with something on your own for whatever reason, then it's smart not to. Part of being confident means knowing when it's time to say "no" or "not yet." If that's how you're feeling, take a break from whatever you're dealing with. Get help if you need it.

Need to Know?

Do Something
www.dosomething.org

This site encourages students to get involved with issues that matter to them. Teens taking the lead in projects concerning animal rights, the environment, safer schools, and other social issues build confidence while making a difference in their communities. Visit the site to learn how you can get involved.

Teens Health
www.teenshealth.org

If your self-confidence needs a boost or you need help silencing the Opinionator, search this site for articles on mental health, feeling sad, being the best you, relationships, and more.

Nobody is totally confident all the time. Not even super-athletes, super-celebs, or the super-popular people in your school. Every once in a while, your Opinionator may try to shake your confidence by telling you that you're "not enough" of something or that you're "too much" of something else.

The truth is, you really are good enough just the way you are. Is it possible to get better? Sure. And it's a good thing to work on improving your health, your attitudes, and your abilities. **But trying to get better doesn't mean that you aren't already a good person who deserves respect.**

You are and you do.

"I READ A PARAGRAPH AT SCHOOL AND I THINK MY TEACHER LAUGHED AT ME BECAUSE OF MY SPEECH PROBLEM. I NEVER ANSWER QUESTIONS ANYMORE BECAUSE I'M AFRAID I'LL BE LAUGHED AT."
—TOM, 11

THIS GUY'S MAKING A BIG ASSUMPTION

WHAT'S AN ASSUMPTION?

SOMETHING YOU ACCEPT AS BEING TRUE WITHOUT ANY PROOF.

ASSUMPTIONS ALMOST KEPT JEN AND ME FROM BEING FRIENDS!

LAST YEAR, DURING PLAY PRACTICE

WE WERE LEARNING THIS DANCE.

HA! HA! HA!

HA!

WE CRACKED UP 'CAUSE

WE WERE BOTH SO BAD!

THEN MICHELLE GAVE ME HALF OF HER CANDY BAR AND THAT SHOCKED ME.

SHE'D NEVER TALKED TO ME, SO I THOUGHT SHE HATED ME.

DID YOU KNOW SHE THOUGHT THAT?

EMILY SAID SHE HATED ME.

I NEVER TOLD EMILY THAT!

SO YOU BOTH ASSUMED THE OTHER PERSON HATED YOU.

GOOD THING YOU'RE BOTH TERRIBLE DANCERS!

Imagine a teacher saying:

"If you don't turn in homework, I'll assume you don't want to do well."

Suppose you're a good student but one day a family emergency keeps you from doing your homework. Your teacher assumes you "don't want to do well"—even though it's not true and it's not fair either.

People make assumptions all the time about a lot of things. You probably assume you'll get warm water when you turn on the faucet marked with an "H." That's a reasonable assumption, based on what's happened in the past. Deciding your next move based on reasonable assumptions makes sense.

But some assumptions, like the one the teacher made, are unreasonable. That's when someone doesn't know enough to be certain what they're saying is true. If you make decisions based on unreasonable assumptions, you may judge yourself or other people unfairly. You may also cheat yourself by refusing to try something new.

THESE KIDS ARE MAKING SOME MAJOR ASSUMPTIONS.

From the "I assume ..." FILES

"I can't make new friends."
—James, 12

"Nobody takes me seriously because I'm tall and blond."
—Hannah, 14

"People hate me."
—Lee, 13

"I can't wear a bathing suit top without padding."
—Danielle, 12

"I am the drama queen of all drama queens."
—Arielle, 13

"The tough guy habit is hard to break."
—Thomas, 14

"I'll never have freedom to do what I want."
—Juan, 13

"Being beautiful can get you anything."
—Adina, 14

"I need to be popular."
—Cal, 11

"I am so mature for my age."
—Amy, 12

ASSUMPTIONS TOOLKIT

Unreasonable assumptions can keep you from seeing and knowing the truth about situations, about yourself and about other people. This toolkit can help you figure out whether you're making a reasonable assumption or an unreasonable one.

1. Name one assumption you have about yourself. Need inspiration? Look at the "I assume . . ." quotes to the left. Let's use the last one as an example. ("I'm so mature for my age.")

2. Ask yourself these questions:

   • **Where did my assumption come from?** ("Adults always tell me how mature I am. Also, I compare myself to other people in my grade.")

   • **How does this assumption help me?** ("It makes me feel kind of superior to other kids my age. It gives me confidence to try things they wouldn't try.")

   • **What problems has my assumption caused?** ("Sometimes I act like I know more than other people, so they think I'm stuck-up. And sometimes they leave me out of things.")

   • **How might things be different if my assumption was wrong?** ("If I wasn't actually 'so mature for my age' I'd feel more free to act like a kid and just have fun. I'd also probably stop calling other people 'immature.' Nobody likes that.")

3. Decide: Do I want to hold on to this assumption? ("Hmm. I'll think about it.")

Maybe you've had a major disappointment or two in your life—like getting rejected by a crush or messing up on a test or during a game. Afterwards you might have made unreasonable assumptions about yourself and your future. Feeling frustrated or embarrassed can make it hard for anyone to think clearly. And these feelings can also make you jump to conclusions without looking at the facts—you might forget all of the things you've done right and focus only on the negative.

When your Opinionator turns up the volume and you start imagining situations turning from bad to worse, it's a good idea to take a break to clear your head. Otherwise you may start to think you're a "loser" or that no one likes you.

THESE KIDS ARE LETTING THEIR ASSUMPTIONS STRESS THEM OUT.

I must be a loser . . .

"When I try to talk to people, I never have anything to talk about. I don't want people to know that I don't have any friends because then they won't want to be my friends."
—Joe, 14

"My friends are prettier than me and way more popular. They have better hair, clearer skin, and are just plain cooler than I'll ever be."
—Leona, 13

"Right now I'm feeling like a pathetic loser because all my friends have girl-friends and I don't."
—Will, 13

"Last week I had a birthday party and it really sucked because no one showed up. It's embarrassing. I wish I could just stay at home forever and not have to go to school."
—Natasha, 11

"I lose all confidence when it comes to girls. I keep believing they'll laugh at me and think I'm a weirdo."
—Ricardo, 13

"I'm not accepted into any of the groups at school. There must be something wrong with me if I can't fit in."
—Danielle, 12

Assumption or Fact?

QUIZ

1. "You can't be yourself and be popular." **A or F**
2. "Tell the truth and people will respect you." **A or F**
3. "Everyone loves chocolate." **A or F**
4. "Only weird people like that kind of music." **A or F**
5. "People who wear glasses are smart." **A or F**
6. "Guys don't like dressing up." **A or F**
7. "Everyone has feelings." **A or F**
8. "People can't control themselves when someone pushes their buttons." **A or F**
9. "Girls can't keep secrets." **A or F**
10. "If I keep trying, I'm going to make it." **A or F**

Answers

1. **Assumption.** You can be yourself and be popular. You can also be fake and be popular. Which way would you rather be?
2. **Assumption.** People won't necessarily respect you if you tell the truth. They won't necessarily respect you if you lie either. But if you tell the truth, you're more likely to respect yourself.
3. **Assumption.** Some do. Some don't. Watch out for statements with "everybody" or "nobody." They're usually unreasonable assumptions. But not always. (See #7)
4. **Assumption.** Judge people based on assumptions and you may miss out on some new friends—and some new music!
5. **Assumption.** Some smart people wear glasses. Some smart people don't. Making assumptions about people based on gender, looks, or how they talk or dress gets in the way of thinking for yourself and seeing people as individuals. (See #6)
6. **Assumption.** Some do and some don't. (See #3 and #5)
7. **Fact.** That's why it's important to pay attention to what you do and say. You don't want to purposely hurt someone's feelings.
8. **Assumption.** Some people have trouble controlling their behavior and some have learned to calm down and think before they react. If you don't let people push your buttons, you're less likely to get pushed around.
9. **Assumption.** Some girls can't keep secrets. Some guys can't either. And some girls and guys keep secrets very well. (See #3 and #6)
10. **Assumption.** You can't prove this one way or another, but here's a fact: If you give up you won't succeed. Sometimes, your assumptions about what you can do provide the energy you need to succeed.

Need to Know?

Do Something
www.dosomething.org
This site is filled with inspirational stories about real teens who aren't stopped by anyone's assumptions about who they are or what they can accomplish.

The InSite
www.theinsite.org
The InSite is filled with tips for doing things your own way while keeping an open mind—without getting swallowed up by other people's opinions.

Assumptions can be reasonable or completely off the wall. It's not always easy to tell the difference, but with practice you can get a lot better. Assumptions have the power to confuse you and make you feel powerless if you let them. When others want to limit you or put you down, remember an important fact:

You and your future are UNLIMITED.

Chapter 6: I Don't Get It

No one wants or expects every day to be just like the one before. (How boring would that be?) But when unexpected things get in your way or stop you cold—like when a short cut turns into a dead end—it's normal to feel confused about what to do next.

You probably don't need anyone telling you that life can be full of surprises. Like when friends suddenly stop acting like friends or adults at home change their minds about what you can or can't do. **Life can quickly become very confusing.**

HERE'S WHAT CONFUSES THESE TEENS.

I get confused when . . .

"I don't get my mother when she buys a third pair of shoes—right after she's said she can't afford $30 to treat my friends for my birthday."
—Lawrence, 13

"I don't know what to do when a guy says he has a crush on me and then stops talking to me."
—Nicole, 14

"What are you supposed to do when someone is mad at you and you don't know why?"
—Marco, 11

"It makes no sense when my guy friend acts so differently around other people than he does with me."
—Natalie, 12

"I'm kinda confused when I think about the future."
—David, 13

"I think I like her, then I don't, then I do."
—Ramon, 13

"I go to a new school and I don't know where all my classes are."
—Dee, 12

Your Next Best Move

When you're confused, you might not be doing your best thinking. Make a decision anyway and you could end up with more problems. Do nothing and you may feel overwhelmed and stuck. So what do you do?

1. **Tell the truth.** Say (or think): "I'm not sure what to do." That's healthier and less stressful than pretending you understand what's going on when you don't.

2. **Calm down.** Breathe. Exercise. Write down your feelings. Talk to a parent or a friend. Whatever works to calm you down is fine as long as it's legal, healthy, and shows respect for yourself and others.

3. **Think about what you want.** Ask yourself, "What's my goal?" Sometimes you may know exactly what you want and sometimes you might not be so sure. (That's part of the confusion!) Before you make your next move, name your goal by thinking, "What do I want?" (Don't go on to #4 until you have an answer.)

4. **Consider your options.** Ask yourself, "What are my options for getting what I want?" Listening to your Opinionator and making snap decisions may not be a great idea. Slow down and think about your options. (You always have at least two.) Make a list.

5. **Choose a plan.** Select the option that is most likely to help the situation.

IMPORTANT. If you can figure things out on your own, great. If you need help deciding what you want or how to get it, though, be sure to ask someone you trust for advice. Don't stop asking until you have the answers you need.

How Confusing!

1. You get a homework assignment that you don't understand. You:
   a) fake it and write something even though you know it's probably wrong.
   b) call a friend in your class.
   c) ask a parent or older sibling for help.
   d) decide not to do the homework.

2. Your friend says a certain guy is annoying. Later, the same day, you see your friend flirting with the "annoying" person. You decide to:
   a) ask your friend what's going on.
   b) say nothing and continue feeling confused.
   c) hang out with your confusion and see what happens.
   d) tell the guy what your friend said.

3. Your coach isn't letting you play much lately and you don't know why. You:
   a) diss the coach.
   b) start skipping practice.
   c) talk to the coach in private.
   d) complain to your teammates.

4. First your parents said you can go to a movie with friends, then they change their minds without giving a reason. You decide to:
   a) call your friends and tell them that you're sick.
   b) sneak out and go to the movies anyway.
   c) stay angry all weekend.
   d) ask your parents why they changed their minds.

5. You just found out your friend lied to you. You:
   a) tell other people what a liar your friend is.
   b) ask your friend straight up, "Why did you lie to me?"
   c) say nothing and stop trusting your friend.
   d) make a list of all the reasons you should and shouldn't confront your friend.

Answers

I. b) or c) 10 points. Asking for help can clear up confusion.

2. a) or c) 10 points. Straight talk can resolve a situation. It's also true that a little mystery won't kill you. You don't want to make big decisions if you're confused about something, but it's okay to not completely understand every single thing. Things might become clearer if you just give it some time.

3. c) 10 points. Getting reliable information can help you understand what's going on.

4. d) 10 points. You may not like your parents' answer, but at least you won't be confused anymore.

5. b) or d) 10 points. Talking to your friend is a good move. But if you're not yet ready to do that, making lists can help you sort out feelings.

Scores

40–50: You aren't afraid to talk directly to people who've got the information you need. You know that's the best way to clear up confusion.

30: You've had some good results asking questions when you're not sure what to do. Try to remember that and you will have more confidence to speak up.

0–20: Speak up more often and you'll feel more in charge of your feelings and actions.

I DON'T KNOW WHAT TO DO!

"My best friend went on vacation and made a new best friend. How could someone become a 'best friend' in about six hours!? We've been best friends for three whole years. I feel left out and hurt."
—Callie, 13

"I got mad at my mom and walked away from her. That made her mad, which is really weird. She's the one that always tells me to walk away when I feel things are going to get really bad."
—Antoine, 11

"One of my good friends started smoking, and she knows that's something I despise. I still want her as my friend but there are things she does that get on my nerves."
—Aisha, 14

"My guy friend has an odor problem. I don't know if I should tell him and help him out or keep it to myself to not hurt him."
—Theresa, 13

"I'm not sure if I should tell my boyfriend that I kissed another boy. I'm scared he'll tell people that I cheated or break up with me and never talk to me again."
—Rachel, 13

"Sometimes I feel like I'm floating in the ocean just looking up at the clouds wondering what the heck is going on!"
—Zeek, 12

WEIGHING Pros & Cons

Confused about whether you should or shouldn't do something?
    Try this:

1. Get a piece of paper and fold it in half the long way.
2. On one side of the page, list all the good reasons for doing whatever it is you're thinking about.
3. On the other half, list all the good reasons for not doing it.
4. When you're done, look over both lists. Which one is longer—the list for doing it or for not doing it?

If your lists are the same length and you're still confused, try this:

1. Imagine that you've gone ahead and done it. What might happen as a result? How do you think you'll feel?
2. Imagine that you don't do it. What might happen as a result? How do you think you'll feel?

Still confused? Get advice from someone whose opinion you respect. If you're still not sure of your best move, decide not to do anything until you feel confident about your choice.

JEN! KNOW HOW TO GET TO THURSTON?

GO DOWN THE HILL AND TAKE THE THIRD LEFT.

THANKS!

WHAT ARE YOU DOING HERE, JEN?

IT'S MY AUNT'S HOUSE. THINGS AREN'T GREAT AT HOME.

WHAT'S UP?

MY PARENTS ARE FIGHTING AND I FEEL KINDA LOST.

DON'T ASK HIM FOR HELP! HE'S MR. "I MAKE SNAP DECISIONS EVEN WHEN I'M TOTALLY CONFUSED."

THAT'S YOUR OPINION.

NO, MAN, I HAVE PROOF.

FAIR ENOUGH.

JEN, YOU DID THE RIGHT THING TO COME HERE.

YOU THINK?

TOTALLY. WHEN YOU'RE CONFUSED, YOU NEED TO CHILL.

THANKS, GUYS!

ANY TIME.

HEY! YOUR AUNT HAVE ANY GOOD FOOD?

YEAH! THAT'S THE OTHER REASON I CAME!

Sometimes you get news that changes your life—like finding out that your parents are getting divorced or hearing that a family member has a serious illness. Other kinds of news can also pull the rug out from under you, like discovering that a friend's been cutting or has a drug problem. Maybe you've been in a tough situation like this before. Maybe you're in one now. It's important to remember that you didn't cause what's going on. It can also help to realize that it's not within your power to undo any of it. What's happened has happened, and it's up to you to help make the best of the situation.

Sometimes it's not news that you're dealing with, but a direct hit— maybe you've been the target of bullying or another form of abuse. In these situations, no one automatically "knows" what to do. **It's normal to feel confused, hurt, or any other emotion. It's even normal to be so shocked that you don't know what you're feeling. Whenever you're overwhelmed by any of life's big challenges, it's important to turn to people you trust for support.**

What I did when I was confused . . .

"One time my dad made a comment I thought was racist. I had never heard him say anything like that before, and it really upset me. I asked him not to say anything like that ever again."
—Cody, 13

"A girl at school sent me a very mean email. It scared me because I thought she might also send it to other people and I'd lose friends. But instead of engaging, I didn't respond or let her know I was upset."
—Zoe, 14

"At a party a friend drank too much and passed out. I wasn't sure what to do, but I decided to call for an ambulance. Everyone else actually tried to stop me from doing anything because they were worried that their parents would find out that they were drinking. But I called and ended up saving my friend's life."
—Karim, 14

"At school these girls started following me around in the halls. They'd split up and whenever I turned a corner I'd meet up with one or two of them. Then the rest would be around the next corner. I was afraid, so I went to the guidance counselor's office to talk with him about it."
—Inga, 11

"My brother and stepbrother are very close. When one of them gets mad at me, they gang up on me in a verbal fight. I talked to my mom and stepdad and they said I should tell the boys how I feel. I spoke with each of them alone—both said they would try harder to stop the fights from happening."
—Brinn, 13

"My mom and dad argue a lot. When I don't say anything, I feel like it's my fault. Lately, I've been asking them to stop doing it around me."
—Bryan, 12

Need to Know?

Being confused is part of life, and it can happen every time there's an unexpected shift from what you're used to. It's not necessarily a bad thing, it just depends on what's causing the confusion and whether you're dealing with everyday challenges or something really serious. Making decisions when you're confused is hardly ever a good idea. That's especially true when you're feeling overwhelmed, scared, or hopeless.

When you're not sure what to do, it's good to remember to:

1. **STOP**
2. **CALM DOWN**
3. **THINK ABOUT WHAT YOU WANT**

And ask for help when you need it. That's a real sign of strength.

FINALLY, I GET TO SHOW MY STUFF!

Student Talent Show TODAY 2 pm!

HEY, EL SHRIMPO! YOU IN THE TALENT SHOW?

WHY DO YOU CARE?

WE LOVE WATCHING PEOPLE MAKE FOOLS OF THEMSELVES.

HA!

HA! HA!

HA! HA!

HEY, MAT! WHAT ARE YOU DOING DOWN THERE?

NERVOUS?

WHAT IF I MESS UP? UGGGH!

You don't need a book to tell you that middle school can be stressful—you're there every day. You know all about the homework, harder classes, and too-many tests. You're probably also busier than ever outside of school, whether it's practice for sports, band, drama, or other activities you might have. A lot of these things are really fun, but a jam-packed schedule can leave you feeling stretched thin. At the same time you're trying to stay on top of things, you also have to sort through family situations and figure out the ever-changing social scene.

What stresses ME OUT

HERE ARE SOME THINGS THAT STRESS TEENS.

"My parents make me crazy because they expect everything I do to be perfect. I'm just a teen who's trying to please everyone and failing horribly."
—Celia, 14

"Everything in my life stresses me out—homework, school, baseball, projects, girls, guys who are jerks—it doesn't end. I have to hide how crazy I feel."
—Danny, 11

"I get upset when people yell at me or call me names. I think anyone would."
—C.J., 12

"It gets to me when teachers expect all this work from you and they don't help you out."
—Ed, 13

"It freaks me out not knowing what skirt to buy. If you wear something to school that other people don't like you can lose friends."
—Nadia, 14

"Sometimes I forget homework assignments until the last minute. Then I have time to worry, but not time to complete them."
—Simone, 12

"My soccer coach stresses me out—I don't like people who scream a lot."
—Diego, 13

"Sometimes I stress myself out by making things seem worse than they really are."
—Jeannie, 13

There's a lot of new ground to cover during middle school, and that kind of change can throw anyone off balance. Not because all of the changes are bad—most are actually great opportunities to try things you've never done before. It's just that new activities and experiences can also cause some uncertainty and leave you doubting that what you're doing is good enough.

Staying on top of schoolwork and other responsibilities can wear out anyone at times. There might be days you don't feel your best—maybe you have some pretty negative thoughts playing in your head or other people are pushing your buttons. Sometimes it might even feel like you're at war with yourself, your close friends, or your family.

All of this adds up to a whole lot of stress. The problem is most people don't notice tension and anxiety building up inside them until they lose control and it's too late. Instead of dealing with the feelings in a healthy way, they often explode or do something without thinking that makes a situation worse. **If you can tune in to that uh-oh-something's-not-right-here feeling, you've got a secret weapon in the form of an early warning system. Use that system to lower your stress before you do something you wish you hadn't and you just might find that things aren't as chaotic or difficult as they seem.**

5 Everyday Ways to DE-STRESS . . . .

1. **Gratitude.** When you're stressed, your Opinionator can flood you with worries and try to make you forget what's right in your life. Don't let it! Instead, take out a piece of paper and write at least five things that are actually okay right now. Your list might include the fact that you've got a caring family, that you scored in the last game, or that there's chicken for dinner. (You get the idea.) Reminding yourself of the big or little things that you appreciate can make you feel less stressed and more in control.

2. **Music.** You probably already know that music can lift your spirits and help you relax. Just listen to a song that you really like and watch what happens to your mood. Feel free to sing along or play air guitar. There's a good chance you'll start feeling better before the song is over. (Warning! Listening to sad or angry songs that reinforce negative feelings can actually make you feel worse.)

3. **Exercise.** A good workout that gets you sweating and your heart pumping is guaranteed to lower your stress levels. Next time you're feeling overwhelmed, try some rapid-fire sit-ups, push-ups, stair-stepping, bicep curls, jumping jacks, or run in place. Exercise can help you relieve the tension in your body and in your brain.

4. **Laughter.** Laughter is a great de-stressor. And the funny thing about it, you don't really need anything to laugh at. Just start by pretending to laugh for 5 to 10 seconds and you just might find that real laughter kicks in. Watch out—once you start you may have trouble stopping! Try this one with your friends or your family and you may have everyone cracking up.

5. **Sleep.** Your body and brain need plenty of rest to help you stay on top of your responsibilities. How much rest? Doctors recommend nine and a half hours of sleep each night. (Most teens only get about seven.) Sleep deprivation can mess with your mood and make it harder to concentrate. Get more sleep every night and you'll be less stressed every day.

Have you ever felt pretty confident about doing something and then suddenly something or someone knocks you off balance? If that's ever happened, then you probably understand what it feels like to go from "I'm ready" to "I can't do this." It's normal be a little anxious when you're facing a new challenge. But if you get so shaken up that you start believing any negative thoughts going through your mind, then it's time to get back in control. You can do this by taking a "breathing break." Afterwards, you'll be in a much better place to figure out your next best move. Breathing breaks can also help when you're feeling rushed or overworked.

How do you relieve stress?

THESE TEENS HAVE OTHER IDEAS FOR REDUCING STRESS.

"I write about whatever's upsetting me. That way I get my emotions out without doing something stupid."
—Carson, 13

"I do Aikido to feel better. My teacher shows us how to find our center and relax."
—Paulo, 12

"I discovered something that works every time I'm really anxious. I wipe my face with cool water and remind myself that I have friends who are there for me."
—Tom, 13

"I talk to my mother. Expressing my feelings makes me feel as though a great burden has been lifted off of my chest."
—Maria, 13

"When I'm feeling crazy, I like listening to jazz or blues music and trying to play it on my guitar."
—Amanda, 13

"The artist I like raps about his life growing up in a rough neighborhood. Hearing other people's stories makes me feel less worried or depressed."
—Bernard, 14

"Doing crossword puzzles calms me down. Then I can deal with whatever is stressing me."
—Ivy, 14

Relax & Re-Center

Reaching out for help is always a great way to reduce your stress. Reaching inside and taking care of yourself can be a huge help, too. Breathing is the fastest way to calm down. Breathing? Yep, that's right, but this is a special kind called re-centering breathing. Here's how it works:

1. **Stop whatever you're doing.** No excuses. Just stop.

2. **Sit down on a chair.** (If you can lie down with a pillow under your knees and your arms at your sides, even better!)

3. **If you're in a chair, put your feet flat on the floor.** Rest your palms on top of your thighs.

4. **Close your eyes.**

5. *Relax* **your hands and fingers, feet and toes.** *Relax* your butt muscles. *Relax* your stomach. *Relax* your shoulders. *Relax* your face, your jaw, your mouth. *Relax* your tongue. Inhale *slowly* and evenly through your nose.

6. **Exhale** *slowly* **and evenly through your mouth.** (Say, *Ahhhhhh.*)

7. **Repeat. Focus on your breathing and nothing else.** Inhale *slowly*. Exhale *slowly*.

8. **Think (don't say) "1" as you inhale and think "1" as you exhale.** Think "2" while continuing the slow, steady breathing. Keep thinking of the next number with each breath (3, 3, 4, 4, etc.). If you lose count, start at 1 again.

9. **Your mind will probably wander.** That's okay. Just notice the thoughts and bring your attention back to your breathing. Start counting at 1 again.

10. **After a few minutes open your eyes and sit there.** Feel less stressed and more centered? If not, close your eyes and breathe some more.

TO BE CONTINUED.

Even if you do your best to keep stress in check, there will still be times when something happens, out of the blue, and you'll get knocked down. Sometimes it might be a serious family situation like parents fighting, money worries, or having to move. Maybe you're struggling to keep up in school and feel a lot of pressure from adults. Or perhaps you're running into difficulties with other students—maybe issues with former friends or bullying so that you don't feel safe or accepted.

Big time stress—whether it's triggered by something out of the blue or it's been building for a while, can make you feel out of control. It can also drive you over the edge in a flash. In that moment you may do or say something that makes your situation much worse. Before you get to that point, take care of yourself and reach out for the help and support of those you trust.

I DIDN'T KNOW WHAT TO DO . . .

"I was very afraid of telling my parents that I'm gay. Even though I acted like everything was okay, I knew I was hiding this big thing from them. I asked my favorite teacher if she knew of any gay youth hotlines that my "friend" could call. She was so caring that I just told her that the person I was talking about was me. I cried and she gave me a hug. Then she gave me the number of a hotline. After I called, I felt much better and even told my parents. They said, 'It's all right. We love you and accept you.'"
—Kathy, 14

"I have been bullied often. Some kids told me that if I didn't give them money they would beat me up. I was very afraid, but I didn't want to tell because I thought they would hurt me worse. I couldn't stand it—I was so worried I couldn't sleep. Finally I told my dad and he called the principal of my school. The boys were suspended, and if they do that kind of thing again, they will be charged."
—Sean, 13

"I was in a gang where I used to live. Things were pretty intense. After I got in a fight, another kid and his cousin were looking for me. I was afraid because the kids were tough—some had been in juvvie. I told my mom that I was afraid and wanted to move. At my new school, some people tried to get me to join a gang but I said no. It isn't worth it."
—Ed, 14

Too Stressed to Think? Staying Sane When Life Makes You Crazy by Annie Fox and Ruth Kirschner. This book offers practical information and stress-reducing tools you can use every day. Learn about the mind-body connection and discover ways to stay cool and make smart choices when the pressure's on.

Stress Relief: The Ultimate Teen Guide by Mark Powell. This book offers ideas for handling stressful situations. Included in the book are meditation and breathing exercises that can be helpful for calming down when the pressure's on.

We'd all like to feel safe and centered all of the time, but that's not always possible.

Whether you're dealing with a short-term situation or long-term stress that you don't have a lot of control over, there are ways to help yourself. The first thing is always to pay attention to what you're feeling. If your warning system tells you that something's not right, then listen to it. That's a way to show respect for yourself. Another way is to reach out to someone you trust. **You may not be able to change everything about the situation you're facing, but you can start to feel better.** You deserve that.

There will probably always be people who try to bring you down. Some may want to make a fool of you so they feel more powerful. Others may just see you as a threat. When people tell you that you're not good enough the way you are, your Opinionator may start to agree. Maybe you'll even feel tempted to act in different ways just to fit some definition of what's "cool." Changing yourself for that reason isn't a long-term solution because someone else can come along and simply change the "rules" for who you should be.

If you're feeling pressure to be someone you're not, it can help to remember that there's only one person in the world who has power over you—you. Only you get to decide how you'll think, act, and feel about yourself. Standing up for what you believe can take guts. After all, it's natural to want to be liked by others, and going against a certain crowd or clique might threaten your social status. But there are always others who will accept and respect you for who you are—people who appreciate all of your great qualities and share your sense of right and wrong.

WHAT'S COOL ABOUT YOU?

You can build confidence when you play to your strengths—what you are, what you know, and what you can do. If you're not sure what all of your strengths are, try this:

1. Imagine you're creating a Web page that's all about you. On your page you have these statements
   I'm cool because I am ...
   I'm cool because I know ...
   I'm cool because I can ...
   How would you finish the sentences? You don't have to limit yourself to just one answer for each. If you have lots of great things about you, make lists.
2. Collect song lyrics or original poetry that fit with what you said in #1.
3. Collect images (photos, drawings, graphics) that also fit.
4. Go ahead and make the Web page—or you can create a collage on paper.

WHAT I LIKE ABOUT MYSELF

I LIKE THAT I DON'T GIVE UP EASILY. HERE'S WHAT THESE TEENS LIKE ABOUT THEMSELVES.

"I don't hide things from friends. I think honesty is a good way to live your life."
—Dev, 14

"I'm outspoken. I talk a lot about how unfairly certain people are treated. It's important to bring up things that need to change."
—Elise, 13

"I like the fact that I'm creative. It helps me all the time in lots of different ways."
—Wen, 13

"I'm a nerd and proud of it."
—Derrick, 11

"I always try to be nice to people, even if they're not the most popular people."
—Caitlinn, 14

"I'm kinda proud of my ability to laugh at myself."
—Carson, 12

"I'm a unique person who doesn't look for anyone's approval."
—Jo-Jo, 13

"I'd have to say that I like my ability to take a bad situation and turn it into an enjoyable time for myself and others."
—Suzanne, 12

"I help people with their problems. I think that's a good thing."
—Ezra, 12

"I am very confident in my own skin."
—Fay, 13

"I give myself top marks on sincerity, compassion, and creativity."
—Brad, 14

"I would say that I am thoughtful of others."
—Celia, 10

"I am open-minded and a good listener."
—Sarah, 12

"I definitely have a sense of adventure. I'm always up for doing new things."
—Peter, 14

Maybe you're the kind of person who already feels pretty confident in yourself most of the time. If not and you could use a little push toward letting your confidence show, think about this: You can inspire others without even knowing it. It's great to see people doing their own thing without worrying about what others think. If you live your life this way, you can show others that they can, too. And you may start to realize that the possibilities for your life are limitless when you don't let others define the limits for you.

That works for me!

"The more you work to be happy, the more 'happiness muscle' you build. Love, accomplishment, appreciation, physical health, and anything else that brings a sense of fulfillment all can help you feel good."
—Leah, 13

"You have to believe that you mean something to someone and that you are loved by people. Open your mind up to that feeling by reaching out to friends, family, and other people you may not be close with now. Get up in the morning, and say, 'I am me, I am special, I am loved.' This actually works—it takes a lot to bring me down."
—Renaldo, 14

"I used to worry about what other people thought of me, and I sometimes still do. But my friends are very unique and they don't care about what others think of them. I guess this influences me to be myself and feel confident in who I am."
—Heather, 12

"Enthusiasm is a biggie. The night before Valentine's Day I wrote eight poems and printed each thirteen times to give me 104 Valentine's cards. The next day I gave them out with total enthusiasm. Anyone could have said, 'You're lame' or 'Get out of my face,' but they didn't. Everyone really liked it. I was on a high for weeks."
—Paul, 11

Are you looking for more ways to build your confidence?
Take a clue from what you like to do. For example, if drawing is your thing, make more time in your day to draw. If you like playing music, start or join a band. Doing things you like can help you feel good about yourself. And because practice makes you better, spending more time on your interests can make you feel more proud of your abilities.

If you haven't yet reached perfection, don't worry. You're part of a club that includes everyone on Earth. But, if something is important to you, putting in the hard work definitely is worth it. **As you make progress, you might realize that NOTHING can stop you from being whatever you want to be.**

4 WAYS TO FEEL GOOD ABOUT YOURSELF

1. **Give to others.** When you give of yourself, you give to yourself a huge vote of confidence. That's the magic of helping others and making a difference in the world. You might find service projects online or through your school, community groups, or at your house of worship.

2. **Set goals.** Determined to pull up your grades? Improve your jump shot? Quit biting your nails? Lose weight? Whatever "self-improvement" dream you have, go for it. Make a plan of action, create a progress chart, and stick with it. Along the way, you'll learn to trust yourself as a person who does what you set out to do.

3. **Forgive yourself.** You're not perfect and sometimes you'll make less than perfect choices. When you've made a mistake, figure out what you've learned, apologize to anyone you hurt, and apologize to yourself. That way you can quit feeling bad and get back in the game of life.

4. **Find real friends.** Hanging out with real friends (the ones you can trust and count on 100 percent) can offer a confidence boost when you're feeling down. Even when you're feeling just fine, real friends provide the total acceptance everyone needs and deserves.

Need to Know?

YMCA and YWCA

www.ymca.net

www.ywca.org

You can find a "Y" in pretty much every part of the country. Visit these Web sites for community opportunities that include athletics, arts education, and teen leadership programs.

Youth Service America

www.ysa.org

Making a difference in your community can make a difference in the way you see yourself. Helping others can help you gain confidence, and you may discover talents and abilities that you never knew you had. Visit this site for opportunities to improve life in your corner of the world.

You can try to be someone else to get others to like you, but it's not going to work. Not really. And why bother when it's so much more fun to be yourself? This is your life, after all — why not start living it as only you know how?

There's only one way to be like them. There are a ZILLION ways to be YOU.

Go for it!

Index

About the Author

Annie Fox, M.Ed., graduated from Cornell University with a degree in Human Development and Family Studies and completed her master's in Education at the State University of New York at Cortland. After a few years teaching in the classroom, she began to explore the ways in which technology could be used to empower teens.

Annie has since contributed to many online projects, including as creator, designer, and writer for the The InSite—a Web site for teens taking on life's challenges. Annie also answers questions for the Hey Terra! feature, an online adviser. Her Internet work has contributed to the publication of multiple books, including *Too Stressed to Think?* and the Middle School Confidential series. Annie is available for public speaking engagements and workshop presentations on teen and parenting issues.

When not answering Hey Terra! letters, Annie enjoys yoga, meditation, cooking, hiking, traveling, and, most of all, spending time with her husband David and the rest of the family.

About the Illustrator

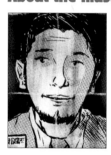

Matt Kindt was born in 1973 to a pair of artistically supportive parents. Living briefly in New York, Matt has spent most of his years in the Midwest, and the last 15 years in Webster Groves, Missouri, a suburb of St. Louis. In middle school, he would often create mini-comics featuring the teachers, to the delight of his fellow classmates. Matt is the Harvey Award–winning writer and artist of the graphic novels *Super Spy* and *2 Sisters* and the comic series *MIND MGMT;* and co-creator of the Pistolwhip series. He has been nominated for four Eisner and three Harvey Awards. In addition to graphic novels, Matt also works as a freelance illustrator and graphic designer. When he is not working, Matt enjoys long trips to the playground with his wife and daughter.

Apps Available!

Developed by Electric Eggplant. Available for the iPhone, iPod Touch, iPad, NOOK, and Android tablets at iTunes (educator discounts available), BN.com, and Amazon.com. To learn more, visit freespirit.com/msc.

Based on the books in the Middle School Confidential series, these apps allow readers to interact with the stories through movie-like sound effects, music, and interactive quizzes.

Available Online
- Free Leader's Guide
  freespirit.com/MSC
- Middle School
  Confidential book video

Be Confident in Who You Are

Real Friends vs. the Other Kind

What's Up with My Family?

Praise for

KNIGHTS
VS
DINOSAURS

INDIE NEXT PICK
KIRKUS BEST BOOK
JUNIOR LIBRARY GUILD SELECTION

"Whether jousting with a triceratops or facing down a T-rex, [squire] Mel should come with a halo: She's thoughtful, sensitive, and wise. . . . Drawn deftly, lightly."
—*New York Times*

"Epic—in plot, not length—and as wise and wonderful as Gerald Morris's Arthurian exploits."—*Kirkus Reviews* (starred review)

"Catnip for kids . . . absurdly entertaining. . . . Gender stereotypes and egos are challenged along with dinosaurs, giving readers a spectacular book that's victorious on all fronts."—*Booklist* (starred review)

"Four braggart knights and one underappreciated squire square off against dinosaurs, all while learning about teamwork and honesty. . . . As the time-traveling knights try to fight their way back to their true place in time, plot twists reveal the heroes' true identities, adding depth to this hilarious slapstick romp."
—*Publishers Weekly* (starred review)

"This rollicking story is suspenseful and silly . . . even reluctant readers will enjoy."
—*School Library Journal* (starred review)

"Phelan crafts a lighthearted romp of an adventure sure to please readers looking for a chapter book full of both action and humor."—*The Horn Book*

MATT PHELAN

KNIGHTS

vs.

DINOSAURS

GREENWILLOW BOOKS
An Imprint of HarperCollinsPublishers

Knights vs. Dinosaurs
Text and illustrations copyright © 2018 by Matt Phelan
First published in hardcover by Greenwillow Books in 2018; first paperback publication, 2019.

The text of this book is set in Iowan Old Style. Book design by Sylvie Le Floc'h

Library of Congress Cataloging-in-Publication Data
Names: Phelan, Matt, author, illustrator.
Title: Knights vs. dinosaurs / written and illustrated by Matt Phelan.
Other titles: Knights versus dinosaurs
Description: First edition. | New York, NY : Greenwillow Books, an imprint of HarperCollins Publishers, [2018] | Summary: With the realm at peace and few dragons about, the Knights of the Round Table are bored, so Merlin sends them to face the most terrible lizards of all—dinosaurs.
Identifiers: LCCN 2018037131 | ISBN 9780062686244 (pbk)
Subjects: | CYAC: Knights and knighthood—Fiction. | Dinosaurs—Fiction. | Adventure and adventurers—Fiction. | Characters in literature—Fiction. | Merlin (Legendary character)—Fiction. | Time travel—Fiction. | Humorous stories. | BISAC: JUVENILE FICTION / Action & Adventure / General. | JUVENILE FICTION / Humorous Stories. | JUVENILE FICTION / Legends, Myths, Fables / Arthurian.
Classification: LCC PZ7.P44882 Kni 2018 | DDC [Fic]—dc23 LC record available at https://lccn.loc.gov/2018037131

20 21 22 23 PC/LSCH 10 9 8 7

 Greenwillow Books

FOR JASPER

CONTENTS

KNIGHTS

vs.

DINOSAURS

CHAPTER ONE

A SLIGHT EXAGGERATION

When Sir Erec thought the whole thing over, he supposed that he shouldn't have said he'd slain *forty* dragons. Four might have been more realistic. He also shouldn't have boasted in front of Merlin, the one person in court smart enough to know that fierce dragons were—more or less—a flagon of hooey.

Now was not the time for reflection, however. A giant rampaging lizard had just tossed Sir Bors into a tree and was bearing down on poor Sir Hector.

Lance time, thought Sir Erec.

But perhaps it would be best to start at the beginning.

The banquet dragged on and on. Tales had been told, fruit had been juggled, songs had been sung (oh, so many songs). But the worst of it was Sharing Time. Each knight who had stumbled back into Camelot over the past few days now stood before King Arthur with a report of his adventures. Sir Erec thought it might never end.

Lancelot, naturally, had performed the bravest deeds; Galahad, the most noble. The rest scrambled for attention with various feats of derring-do, most of which were exaggerated, to say the least.

The knights all shared a deep secret. With the realm at peace, the knights spent a good deal of their time off in a field somewhere fighting *one another*. Not to slay, just for the sheer fun of it. They had armor and weapons after all. It was a shame not to use them.

Dragons, giants, trolls, and mythical beasts were in short supply. All knights believed in them without question, of course, but the pesky creatures couldn't exactly be counted on to make an appearance. Ever.

So the knights embellished. One tale after another of

battles with beasties, run-ins with rogue trolls, or fisticuffs with fierce giants.

Erec sighed. He was tired. His tunic was slightly scratchy. Whatever the reason, when it was his turn to share, out it came in a loud, clear voice. A whopping big embellishment to shame the rest.

"Did you say *forty* dragons?" asked Merlin with an air of polite interest.

"Yes," declared Sir Erec.

The Round Table exploded with excitement. Knights spouted support or disbelief or a combination of both.

All but the Black Knight. If you needed a tall, dangerously silent type, he was your man. No one had ever heard a peep from the Black Knight. Tonight, as always, he stood in a dark corner in full armor. He stayed rigid, staring at Erec through his visor and helm.

Queen Guinevere spoke, instantly silencing the hall.

"That is a most amazing accomplishment, Sir Knight. Have you no trophy for your king?" she asked.

Oh, dear, thought Erec. "Um," he began. "You see, milady, it was quite dark in the cave and—"

"The cave?" Merlin interrupted. "Where is this cave?"

"Far. Pretty far away actually."

"Oh," said Merlin, folding his napkin. "It is not the cave I am thinking of. Surely you would have not been so fortunate in that particular cave."

It was subtle, but the famous Merlin bait hung in the air. Merlin nibbled a carrot, waiting.

"Of what cave do you speak?" demanded Erec. He had no choice, really. This was all part of the act. If a dangerous adventure was dangled in front of you, a knight must respond.

Merlin cleared his throat.

"Oh, you don't want to know. For in this cave lives the

most fearsome creature of all: The Terrible Lizard."

"Lizard, eh?" said Erec. "I shall go and slay this Terrible Lizard!"

Sir Bors slammed a fist onto the table. "Nay! I shall slay it! Leave brave Sir Erec to rest after such a *noble* feat of slaying *forty* dragons."

The fever spread. Knights were a competitive bunch.

"I, too, should like to best this heretofore unknown creature!" piped Sir Hector, who had an interest in new and exciting beasts.

The Black Knight stepped forward. A hush fell over the room. A creaky nod of his helmet announced he would also join the fun.

Sir Erec rose and turned to King Arthur.

"My liege, with your permission, I shall face this Terrible Lizard." Erec looked back at Bors, Hector, and the Black Knight. "With these three coming along, I suppose."

Arthur poked at a stray pea on his plate. He often tuned out when the knights became overly excited.

"As you wish, brave knights. Mind the people, though."

"Of course, sire! Only the fearsome brute."

"Brutes," corrected Merlin. "There may be a few, come to think of it."

"The more the merrier," quipped Sir Bors. He was not exactly funny, but he often came up with a witty line at a crucial or dangerous moment.

Sir Erec gazed longingly at his mutton. But the deed was done. He had to make a show of it.

"I am off to prepare. I shall leave at first light."

"You will have the cave's location at dawn," said Merlin. "Bring no horses or squires into the cave. You may of course pack a weapon or two. Your choice." He smiled. His gray eyes sparkled.

"Splendid," said Sir Erec, but it came out less booming than he had hoped. The weekend was off to a poor start.

CHAPTER TWO

ADVENTURE, MERLIN STYLE

As the sun rose, Sir Erec perused the directions to the cave, which had appeared at his bedside. He then donned his armor with help from his squire, Derek. It took some time. Derek was more enthusiastic than he was skilled. For this reason Sir Erec usually left his squire at home when he went adventuring. Following Merlin's rule about not bringing a squire into the cave would not be an issue.

After a great deal of clanging, strapping, and adjusting, Erec was ready. Carrying his favorite broadsword and

shield, he clanked his way to the stables.
Sir Hector was already there, looking
quite trim and rested. His garments
were always rather clean despite his
numerous claims of adventures. Still,
Hector, aside from suspicious cleanliness, was not a bad
fellow. It could have been worse.

Then there was Bors. He was worse. A brute in shining
armor, Bors was a Might Makes Right man through and
through. Might Makes Right was the
philosophy that if you could
pound something harder than
the next person, then you
should do as you please. King
Arthur had been doing his
best to dissuade his knights of
this idea, but old habits die hard.

Bors's squire, a thin lad named Mel, struggled with the
knight's many weapons. He carried swords of all sizes, a
mace, a bludgeon, a lance, a shield, several knives, and

even a few rocks. Bors believed in being prepared for any and all encounters.

"Sir Erec!" bellowed Bors. "A fine day to smite a treacherous lizard, eh?"

"*Terrible* lizard, Bors," said Erec. "Get the name right. You don't want to confuse the minstrels later. Also, remember that my name is spelled with two *E*'s. The minstrels will need to know that as well, since I shall be the slayer."

"And you will not be alive to spell it yourself, I wager!" countered Bors.

Hector chuckled. "Good one, Bors!"

Erec simmered.

"It is very early in the morning," he said. "I will furnish a retort in fine wit momentarily."

THUNK!

A great ax chopped through a block of wood, startling the knights, the horses, and several chickens.

The Black Knight lifted the ax and regarded the knights. He turned and swept onto his midnight-black steed.

"Of course a witty retort is not always necessary," mumbled Erec.

"Mel!" barked Bors. "Load the weapons horse and follow me."

"Sir Bors, we are to leave our squires," said Hector.

"My squire is required as far as the cave. He will then tend to our horses. Did none of you think of that?"

Erec and Hector looked at each other. They shrugged, their armor creaking slightly.

"Looks like I'll be doing the thinking for this adventure," said Bors.

"Marvelous. This is getting better and better," Erec grumbled to Hector.

Erec snapped his reins and led the others to the gate. Hector followed, trying to jockey to the front. Bors took his horse to the left in an attempt to pass them both.

The Black Knight rode silently and steadily behind them with nothing to prove whatsoever.

"Yonder is the cave," announced Hector, pointing to a shale hillock with a small opening near the crest.

"Is that not the cave of Reginald the Hermit?" asked Bors.

"No," replied Hector. "Reginald the Hermit moved last summer. He wanted something with a nice view by a lake."

"Silence," commanded Erec. "We shall leave the horses here and proceed on foot. We know not the manner of this beast and must approach with caution."

"You would know, oh, great dragon slayer." Bors snickered. "I will approach on foot, but not because you suggested it. I thought of that moments ago."

"I, too, had created a similar strategy," piped Hector.

The Black Knight dismounted in silence.

The cave entrance was unremarkable. It was just wide enough for the four knights to enter single file, as they did in the following order: Sir Erec, the Black Knight, Sir Hector, and Sir Bors.

CLANG!

Oh, and Mel, Sir Bors's squire.

Mel carried a large, bulky canvas sack filled with weapons. It was the lance that gave him trouble at the entrance.

Erec looked back, annoyed.

"Bors, Merlin said no squires."

"Who will carry my weapons, then? I for one prefer to be prepared. Also, I have difficulty choosing sometimes."

"But Merlin—" Hector began to speak.

"Oh, Merlin! All talk that one with his rules and little tests. You never see Merlin slaying a dragon, do you? What does he know about anything?"

As if in answer, four torches suddenly ignited, lighting a passage deeper into the cave.

"Let's continue on," Erec said. He pulled his sword from its scabbard.

They followed the path and emerged in a small chamber of solid rock also lit by torches. A flat stone sat in the center of the chamber. On it was a large leather-bound book.

"This, uh, seems to be the end of the cave," said Erec, poking the wall with his sword.

"Perhaps the Terrible Lizard stepped out for a bite," said Hector.

"Well, it left its book," said Erec, poking the book with his sword.

"It can read?" asked Hector.

"*I* can't even read, you dunderhead!" snapped Bors.

"Who are you calling a dunderhead?" demanded Hector. "I can read beautifully. My father believed a knight should be well rounded."

Hector inspected the book.

"It has a title: *The Terrible Lizards.*"

"Merlin sent us to slay a book?" growled Bors.

Hector opened the book. A strong wind blew through the cave and extinguished the torches.

Darkness. Silence.

"Well, it certainly seems to be Merlin's book," observed Erec.

A tentative voice came from the entrance to the chamber.

"Sirs?"

"What is it, squire?" barked Bors.

"Only that . . . you see . . . there's a tree outside the cave."

"So?"

"Well . . . it wasn't there before."

The Black Knight strode back down the passage. The other knights followed. At the mouth of the cave they stood stock-still for a moment. Then the Black Knight drew his enormous broadsword from its scabbard.

Directly outside the cave were the tops of tall vine-covered trees. Below spread a lush forest, overgrown with large ferns and moss. To the west, a barren land of dirt and dust and enormous rock formations.

"Merlin," said Erec.

"Merlin," gulped Hector.

"Merlin!" growled Bors.

The Black Knight pointed to the book in Hector's hands.

"Yes. Right," Hector said. "Perhaps there is some guidance here." He began to page through the book.

Erec gazed at the unfamiliar terrain.

"It must be an illusion. See if it says how to break the spell."

"'*Ty-ran-no-saurus rex,*'" read Hector slowly.

"*Rex?*" Erec interrupted. "That means king. A *tyrant* king. Splendid. It's a mission. We take care of this tyrant king and the illusion fades. Let's go."

"*Erm* . . . ," muttered Hector.

"Close the book, Hector. Look lively," said Bors.

Hector closed the book. But he did not look particularly lively.

CHAPTER THREE

TERRIBLE LIZARDS

The entire landscape had changed. Behind them the cave itself was the same, but the shale hillock was now much steeper and surrounded by more rocky hills. As the knights descended, they entered a forest unlike any they had ever seen. Actually it resembled *all* the forests they'd ever seen trying to occupy the same space. It was not an orderly English wood.

"Where are the horses?" exclaimed Hector.

"The horses? Where is Camelot? Where is *England?*"

Erec's voice rose with each inquiry.

"Trickery and illusion," declared Bors. "Mel, my sword. You all wish you brought *your* squires into the cave now, eh?"

Mel reached into the canvas sack and fetched a fine sword.

"I shall explore the perimeter." Bors shut his visor. "Fear me, all who dwell h—"

Bors did not have a chance to finish his bellow. A tremendous creature burst from the trees and snatched

him up in its mighty jaws. The beast lifted Bors twenty feet off the ground and shook him like a puppy's chew toy. Fortunately Bors's armor held.

Sir Erec had seen some surprising things in his day. He'd been ambushed a time or two by barbarians hiding in trees. The Lady of the Lake had waved to him on one occasion. But nothing compared with what he now witnessed. This creature—calling it a lizard was a bit of a stretch although it was clearly reptilian—had a ridge of spikes that ran along its neck and back. It stood on two legs with nasty-looking claws at the end of its long arms. Its jaws held rows of teeth unlike any Erec had ever seen. They crunched into Bors's armor, denting deeper and deeper with each angry chomp.

Bors shouted from within the massive monster's jaws, kicking furiously.

The Black Knight was the first to remember that they were trained knights and leaped into the fray. A broadsword to the lower leg made the creature toss Bors aside.

Sir Erec swung his sword high and aimed for the tail, but the monster was fast for its size. The tail whipped around. Erec attempted to duck, but unfortunately a knight in armor is not the swiftest fighter. Sturdy, yes. Swift, no.

One swat from the tail sent Erec into the air. He landed on Bors.

"Get off me, Sir Knight!" barked Bors. "My honor has been . . . dented!"

Erec rolled over and took in the scene. Hector was off to the side, frantically paging through Merlin's book.

"Hector, what are you doing? Drop that book and engage!" yelled Erec.

The Black Knight had been cornered. The creature snapped its jaws.

"Ah! Here, beast!" Bors hollered, scrambling to his feet.

The monster spun, sprang into the air, and landed a few feet in front of Bors and Erec.

Hector placed the book safely by a rock, drew his

sword, and attacked from behind.

"Mind the fiery breath!" he shouted.

"It doesn't *need* fire!" countered Erec.

The Black Knight jumped in and stabbed at the monster's leg. It roared and swung around wildly, its thick, scaly tail sweeping across the area and easily knocking all four brave knights over like so many bowling pins.

They toppled through a thick brush and over a hidden precipice. One by one they tumbled down into a ravine below with a great deal of . . .

CLANG!
CLANG!
CLANGING!

The Terrible Lizard roared from the top of the slope. It looked, it sniffed, it tried a toe over the edge of the ravine, but then it thought better of the idea. With one final thrash of its tail, it was gone.

The battle had taken scarcely five minutes, but the knights' armor was more dented and scraped than it had been in the past five years of derring-do.

"What in Lancelot's name was that?" yelled Bors.

"Definitely *not* a dragon." Erec rose shakily and removed his helmet.

"Clearly not," said Bors. "In all my years I've seen one—well, obviously *several*—dragons but none that size."

"Or shape," said Hector.

"Or temperament," added Erec.

Mel slid down the hill dragging the sack of weaponry and holding Merlin's book.

Hector perked up. "Well done, squire! The book might—"

"Hang the book, Hector!" Erec said, wiping his sword with his tunic. "It's pretty clear. We have our Terrible Lizard to slay. Then we find this tyrant king fellow, make him bow to Arthur, and end this wretched spell! We don't need to read about it."

"Agreed," said Bors. "And the sooner the better. Squire! I'm in need of a bandage for my arm."

Mel looked stricken.

"I did not bring our supplies, Sir Bors. Only the weapons."

"No matter. Tear me a bandage from your tunic. In addition to this land looking entirely different, we seem to be experiencing the summer months. You will be fine."

"Perhaps one of these fronds or leaves would do better. They are quite sizable, my lord."

"I don't want a leaf!"

"I could find some herbs to go with it. A nice salve or natural ointment."

"I haven't got all day if you haven't noticed, boy! Your shirt! Bandage! Now!"

"No, my lord."

The knights all turned to stare at the squire.

"Did you say *no?*" Bors's complexion went from dark to torrential.

"I'm sorry, sir. I cannot."

Mel clutched his tunic as Bors straightened to his full, intimidating height.

"I'm . . . I'm a girl, Sir Bors."

It had been a strange day. All four knights would have admitted that. And yet this new revelation was in its way even more startling than the events of the last several minutes.

"You're a what now?" growled Bors.

"A female. A girl. A squire still! But a girl squire."

Bors strode over to Mel. She quivered but held her ground.

Bors looked at her for a long moment.

He opened his mouth to speak.

He closed it again.

Then Bors turned and walked over to a rock to sit down.

"That's just wonderful. England is gone. We are facing a monster of epic strength. There's a mysterious tyrant king. And now my squire is a girl. Great. Fantastic.

Anyone else here a *girl*?"

The question was meant to be rhetorical.

But the Black Knight raised a hand.

CHAPTER FOUR

MORE TERRIBLE LIZARDS

The Black Knight stood without a helmet for the first time in anyone's memory. And it was true. The Black Knight was indeed a woman.

The others remained as silent and still as stone. No one so much as blinked.

The Black Knight spoke in a calm, measured tone. "My name is Magdalena. I am the daughter of Robert the Blacksmith. I have wielded a smith's hammer since the age of two. I've swung a sword since age four. I have kept my identity a secret not out of fear or shame. I simply did not wish to deal with the stupidity of other knights."

She drew her sword slowly.

"But now we are no longer in our Age, and we are most likely to die battling this infernal beast. Not that I mind that part. But I see no point in keeping up the ruse of my identity for you lot. So if anyone has a problem, let us discuss it with our weapons."

Still, no one moved.

Eventually Erec found his tongue.

"I think—I think we're all—I mean, *I* don't need to fight you. Personally. Anyone else?"

"No! No!" chirped Hector.

Bors eyed the Black Knight. She towered over him, her sword ready.

"I have other fights to fight," muttered Bors.

"Let's move on then, shall we? We still have a tyrant king to find," said Erec, getting to his feet.

The knights marched into the woods. Bors led the way without a look back at the others. Mel heaved the sack of weapons and followed, glancing back at the Black Knight in awe. Helmet on but visor raised, Magdalena brought up the rear.

They walked in silence except for the unavoidable creaking and clanking of armor. Erec felt slightly dizzy. Whether it was due to the battle with the lizard, the tumble down the hill, the fact that he hadn't had much to eat that day, or that he now found himself in the company of two people of the female persuasion, he could not say. It was a potent mix; that was for sure.

After a few minutes the knights entered a large clearing. There were strange, enormous flowers. There were buzzing insects (also strange and enormous). There was grass.

And there were several giant beasts grazing on the grass in the distance.

Bors raised his sword.

"Wait," whispered Hector.

The creatures continued to graze. A few lifted their heads to regard the knights with mild interest.

"They appear to be docile," continued Hector. "Like a herd of cows."

"Monstrously sized cows," added Erec.

"How many kinds of terrible lizards are there?" asked Bors.

"A bookful, it seems," said Erec.

Smiling, Hector turned to face the company.

"But not all bad! You see? Just very large cows!"

One of the "cows" snorted. It lowered its head. Thick

horns protruded from its crown. It pawed the dirt. Others began to do the same.

"I think they might be *bulls*, Hector," said Erec, lowering his visor.

"Hmm?" Hector still had his back to the beasts. He looked over his shoulder just as the creatures burst into a stampede that shook the ground.

"Ah! Attacking cows! Attacking cows!" screamed Hector, fumbling for his sword.

Mel ducked behind a boulder as the herd came thundering toward them. They made an uncanny, high-pitched screech. It was no moo.

The knights scattered. Erec was knocked aside. Bors tripped over Erec's leg. His sword flew straight up, then came back down. Bors, eyes bulging, shifted just as the sword struck the ground an inch from his cheek.

Hector, blinded in a cloud of dust, swung his sword wildly.

The Black Knight had managed to wrestle one of the creatures to the ground and was pulling hard on its horns. It let out an ear-piercing shriek.

And a deep, rumbling bellow answered from the nearby woods. Birds took flight. Even the bulls paused.

"That does not sound good," said Erec.

The tree line exploded. Trunks crashed to the ground. An enormous monster rammed its way through. Its head was attached to a long, long neck of sheer muscle. Its tail whipped and took down three trees. The roar was deafening. The behemoth's front legs came crashing down like sledgehammers.

The bulls turned away from the pesky knights to face this more serious opponent. They charged at the giant.

"Retreat!" shouted Erec.

The Black Knight grabbed Mel and pushed her along.

The knights made for the trees. A pack of the spiky-spined terrible lizards burst onto the scene directly in front of them.

"Other way!" yelled Hector, tripping over Bors, who clanged into Erec, who slammed into the Black Knight.

The lizards sniffed the air. Unimpressed by the bumbling

knights, they joined the ongoing mayhem, fighting both behemoth and monster bulls with apparent glee.

The knights and Mel took the opportunity to run as fast as they could, not daring to stop until they were deep into the cover of the woods.

Safe. For the moment.

CHAPTER FIVE

TERRIBLE KNIGHTS

ONK!

Bors's armored fist came down on Sir Erec's helmet.

"What was that for?"

"Getting in my way!"

"*Your* way? You were in my way, you oaf!"

"*Oaf?*"

"Do you prefer *lummox?*"

Bors shoved Erec. Erec shoved Bors.

Hector tried to break it up and was kicked in the

shin for his effort. So he kicked back instead.

They pushed. They slapped. They fell over. It was clanging and awkward.

"If I were alone, I would have smited all of the creatures with ease!" said Bors.

"Smote," corrected Hector.

"Watch it, bookworm," Bors said, turning to Hector.

"You think you'd be better alone?" shouted Erec. "I know I would! I'm the king of alone! I adventure solo! No squire! No companions! No irritating, clumsy oafs to trip over!"

"Oaves," corrected Hector.

"*Oaves* is not a word. I can read, too, Hector," snapped Erec.

Magdalena sighed and sat on a fallen tree trunk. Mel dropped the sack of weapons. She looked at the Black Knight. Magdalena indicated the trunk with a wave of her hand. Mel joined her.

"Thank you, sir, um, ma'am," said Mel.

The Black Knight glanced at Mel and then spit a bit of blood onto the ground.

Bors swung out a leg and knocked over Erec.

"Might Makes Right!" shouted Bors.

"Why don't you Might Makes Right yourself out on your own, then?"

"I will indeed!" said Bors, slamming his visor shut. "You all are slowing me down. I'll have this tyrant king defeated by nightfall."

"I, too, shall go off alone!" chimed in Hector. "It will give me a chance to read Merlin's book, which might provide a clue to getting out of this mess. A fact that you knights are too dense to see."

"Reading a book is not going to help. But please feel free to find yourself a nice comfy spot somewhere," said Erec. "The rest of us will search for and deal with this king. Are we all agreed to venture on our own, then?"

They all turned to the Black Knight. The Black Knight had already left.

Bors yanked some weapons from his sack and stalked into the trees.

Hector, with the book strapped to his back, charged in a different direction, sword in hand.

Erec dusted off his armor. He glanced up. Mel was still sitting on the fallen tree. He looked around. They were alone.

"Splendid," Erec muttered. "Come along then."

He headed into the trees. Mel lifted her sack and set off after him.

CHAPTER SIX

TRICERA-JOUST

Sir Erec trudged through the woods with Mel trailing behind him. He stopped abruptly, unbuckled his leg armor, and tossed it aside.

Mel reached for the armor.

"Leave it. It's just slowing me down. Besides, you are *not* my squire," said Erec.

Mel nodded.

Erec continued at a faster pace. Mel tried to keep up.

Erec glanced back. Mel met his eye, then looked away quickly.

Erec sighed.

"So . . . have you always been a girl?"

"Yes, sir."

"Hmm."

They walked some more in awkward silence.

"What about your name? Is it truly Mel?"

"I shortened it from Melancholy."

"*Melancholy*. Cheerful."

"I *am* a good squire, sir."

They left the cover of the woods and entered a dusty clearing.

"I didn't want to be a scullery maid or a serf's wife or a—"

Erec held up a hand. He sniffed the air. He glanced around.

"It's not that I don't find your tale fascinating. And to be perfectly honest, I see your point. But I believe we are not alone."

"Yes, sir."

A brutish creature meandered into the clearing. It was sturdy and solidly built, standing a few feet taller than Erec and measuring the length of a large cart. It had a shieldlike crest over its eyes and three serious-looking horns protruding from its head. Each horn was the length of a sword.

The creature saw them and snorted. It squawked. It took a few steps closer. It squawked more loudly. It waited. Then it narrowed its eyes and lowered its head, taking aim with its three horns.

"Squire—" said Erec.

Mel was already holding out a short lance.

"Excellent choice."

Erec moved into the clearing to face the brute. The beast eyed him but did not charge.

Erec stepped closer, lance raised and ready.

"I've seen worse than you. Wouldn't mind a good horse at the moment, but it can't be helped."

Erec got into position.

"Come now, terrible lizard with pointy weapons, what say you to a bit of sport?"

The creature charged. Erec charged. His lance hit the creature directly between the eyes. The beast grunted, veering off to the side.

"Ha! I wish Arthur could have seen that! Or better yet,

Guinevere." Erec grinned at Mel and winked.

Mel nodded and pointed. "Sir, I think you'd best—"

The beast circled back again. Erec snapped into action. This time the creature deflected Erec's lance and scooped him off the ground. It shook him once, twice, three times, then tossed him aside like a twig.

Erec landed with a thud. Dust swirled around him. When he raised himself to a sitting position, a knight-shaped imprint was left in the dirt behind him.

The three-horned monster squawked and charged from across the clearing.

Erec's lance had landed several yards away. Mel ran for it, but she would never reach it in time.

Erec looked around quickly. A few feet away was a fallen log about the size and length of himself. He dived toward it.

He planted his boots firmly on the ground. He put his shoulder into the log. It was heavy, but Erec put all his strength to the task. It lifted.

Erec held until the very moment the creature was upon him and then:

"Ha!" shouted Erec. He admired his work.

The log creaked under the weight. The beast growled.

Mel cleared her throat. "Sir, perhaps we should take advantage of this moment and—"

"Run?" asked Erec.

"Yes, sir."

"I concur."

They ran into the woods and soon found shelter behind some large rocks. They sat and caught their breaths.

After a moment Erec spoke.

"My squire is worthless, you know."

He looked at Mel and smiled.

"Bors is lucky to have you."

CHAPTER SEVEN

SIR HECTOR AND THE
FEARSOME CHICKENS

Sir Hector had been trekking alone in the forest for some time without incident. He was uncomfortably warm but still in one piece.

When he came upon a secluded clearing with a nice inviting rock, it seemed perfect for a little sit-down.

He surveyed the entire clearing.

He poked the overgrowth with his sword.

It appeared to be lizard free.

Hector put his sword and shield down by the rock.

He unstrapped Merlin's book from his back, pausing a moment to admire the leather binding.

"I don't care what the others think. This book must be important. And I for one am going to read it."

He settled comfortably, opened the book, and began to read.

Hector turned the pages with a mixture of awe, horror, and excitement.

"Fascinating. Just fascinating," he muttered.

He read and read, flipping pages, going back and forth, making noises like "hmm" and "oooh" and "gadzooks."

"They are rather incredible, really. So much variety, too."

The bushes rustled.

Hector looked up.

A twig snapped.

He slowly reached for his sword.

A small creature hopped into the clearing. It was the size of a chicken. It even had feathers of many bright colors. But it also had the scaly head of a reptile.

Large, inquisitive eyes blinked at Hector. It tilted its head and chirped. For a terrible lizard, it was adorable.

"Hello!" said Hector gently.

The chicken took a step back.

"It's all right, my small friend. I won't harm you."

Hector put the book down and inched toward the shy creature.

"There, there. That's a good chicken. Don't be frightened of old Hector. I am a Knight of the Round Table."

Hector reached out slowly.

The chicken let him stroke its head gently. It almost seemed to be smiling.

"That's right. That's right, my little friend."

The chicken closed its eyes and made a little purring noise.

Then it locked its little jaws around Hector's finger, clamping down *hard* with a row of tiny razor-sharp teeth.

"*Yowwww!*"

He shook his hand, but the chicken would not let go.

Hector fell backward. He looked up in time to see another chicken sailing through the air, teeth bared, before it landed on his head.

"*Eeee!*"

Hector rolled over, swatting wildly. The two chickens jumped off and regrouped. The first chicken opened its cute little mouth and whistled shrilly.

Suddenly the bushes exploded with chickens. Hector was completely surrounded.

He looked about him uneasily. He lifted the book. For a long moment nothing moved.

And then the chickens snapped simultaneously into action.

"*Ack!*" Hector swung the book, knocking chickens into the air.

Even more appeared to take their place. Hector tripped

and was instantly set upon by the tiny, vicious cuties. They scratched, nibbled, and pecked the noble knight.

His opinion of the creatures soured considerably.

CHAPTER EIGHT

SIR BORS AND THE MACE-TAILED MENACE

Bors swung his sword with a fierce and mighty roar.

CRACK! CRACK!

The tree didn't stand a chance.

"Arrr!"

Bors kicked the tree for good measure.

He was frustrated. This was unusual. And bothersome. Bors liked to know where he stood. He had no patience for magic and spells. He had no tolerance for boy squires becoming girl squires. Or always being girl squires but tricking him. *Tricking* Sir Bors!

"*Arrrrrrrr!*"

He smote the tree once more.

What he needed right now was a good old-fashioned brawl. He needed a terrible lizard.

As if in answer, a low bark sounded in the near distance.

Bors crashed through the overgrown ferns. Before him stood a four-legged creature. Built low to the ground. Strong legs. Small head. Heavily armored back.

It hissed at Bors.

"Oh, you want to have a go, eh? *Right!*"

The creature thundered up to him, turned sharply, and whomped Bors with its tail. The end of the tail was shaped like a large, rounded stone.

Bors reeled back but quickly recovered. He admired the tail.

"A mace man, eh? Fine!"

Bors reached for his belt. His trusty mace was still there.

Bors and the mace-tailed menace squared off.

They burst into action at the same moment, bludgeoning and punching, biting and kicking. A tremendous cloud of dust obscured the frenzy of action.

Bors swung, but the beast avoided the blow and cracked him again with its tail.

Bors pivoted and conked it on the head.

The creature grunted, shook its head, and plowed into Bors with its plated skull. Bors took it in the gut and fell backward onto his bottom.

He regarded the terrible lizard.

The terrible lizard regarded Bors.

It snorted.

Bors snorted.

Bors rose slowly and raised his mace. The creature raised its tail. And they went at it again.

The beast knocked Bors to the ground. It rose up on its hind legs to crash down, but Bors rolled out of the way and grabbed hold of the tail. The terrible lizard swung him to and fro but could not shake the brave knight.

"You—ah . . . *gah!*"

A cacophony of gut-wrenching roars and shrieks rang from beyond the clearing. Both Bors and the mace-tailed menace paused in midfight.

Trees toppled as five vicious, biting, extra-terrible lizards thrashed their way onto the scene. They tore and bit and kicked one another so intently that they didn't even notice Bors and his opponent.

The mace-tailed lizard charged into the fracas.

Bors watched.

He smiled.

"Wait for me! Huzzah!"

CHAPTER NINE

MIGHT MAKES RIGHT

Sir Erec's and Mel's respite had been short-lived. Currently they were racing through the forest at top speed.

"Don't look back! Don't look back! Don't look back!" called Erec.

They crashed through some thick foliage and tumbled down a steep hill.

Erec scrambled to his feet and peered back up the hill. Nothing. They'd escaped.

"All clear," he said, just as Hector burst out of the

bushes and collided with both Erec and Mel.

"Hector! What the—" Erec started to speak.

"Shh!" Hector was wild eyed and twisting back in the direction he'd come.

Three chicken-size lizards zipped out of the forest and perched on a rock.

They all stared at the creatures for a moment.

"You've got to be kidding, Hector."

The chickens bared their teeth and growled.

"They're rather worse than they look," whispered Hector.

A shield appeared, blocked the sun momentarily, and came down on the chickens from behind with a WHUMP.

The Black Knight lifted the dazed chickens off the rock and tossed them far into the woods.

"Thanks," said Hector.

She turned back to the knights. Her armor was scratched, dented, and muddied. Otherwise she looked just fine.

"Any, uh, trouble with terrible lizards out there on your own?" asked Erec.

"You should ask them," answered the Black Knight, wiping her sword clean.

The area was secure for the moment. Erec, Hector, and Magdalena rested in the shade. Mel organized the sack of weapons.

Hector opened the book.

"I've had a chance to peruse most of the book. It is absolutely fascinating. The illumination work is also quite accurate. I did not know that Merlin was such an artist."

"I have heard that Merlin has enchanted an owl to both write and draw," said Mel.

"Bah." Erec cut in. "Enchant an owl to draw?"

"He enchanted *us* to this wretched place. I should think he could manage to teach an owl to draw," said Magdalena.

"At any rate"—continued Hector—"these terrible lizards are extraordinary in all ways. They're not dragons exactly—"

"They're knights!"

It was Bors. He was standing at the edge of the clearing, bloody and wild eyed with excitement. It was

not often that Bors's mind formulated an insight of any kind. He was on fire with the thrill of enlightenment.

"It's true!" He bounded up to the others.

"They fight us. They fight each other. They fight to conquer, to eat, and, I think, to have *fun*! They have armor, and their claws and teeth are as sharp and true as any blade. Knights! You see?"

"Knights?" said Erec dubiously.

"*Perfect* knights," asserted Bors.

"Whom do they serve?" asked the Black Knight.

"That's the best part." Bors chuckled. "They serve none but themselves. Might Makes Right. Proof in the pudding."

"Might Makes Right. Arthur says Might should be used only in service of the greater good," stated Erec. It was Arthur's guiding principle, and Erec agreed with him.

"Well, perhaps our king is misguided on that point," said Bors.

Mel drew her breath in sharply.

"How dare you." Hector stood.

"If you see Arthur, let me know. But in case you haven't noticed, Camelot is *not here*."

Bors stomped up to Hector and leaned into him face-to-face.

"We are knights. They are knights. We are

pitted against each other fairly. Together we show them who is stronger."

Bors leaned in closer.

"Might. Makes. Right."

Thunderous roars tore through the charged air. The group froze. The roars trailed off into dead silence.

"Where did that come from?" asked Erec.

"*Everywhere,*" said Mel quietly.

They drew their weapons silently. Each knight looked in a different direction. Mel crept behind a boulder.

"Maybe they're gone," said Hector.

Then a tree crashed down beside him, and all was thrown into chaos.

Terrible lizards of all shapes and sizes roared and gnashed teeth and chomped at one another. Great tails swung out. Enormous clawed feet pounded the ground.

And then they noticed the knights. That was when things really got started.

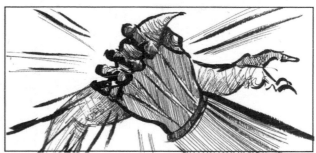

RETREAT!

The knights and Mel ran for their lives.

The ferns gave way to a rocky landscape. Hills of stone rose up everywhere. In a wall of solid rock there was one narrow crevice.

"In here!" shouted Erec.

The knights squeezed through the opening in single file. Sparks flew as their armor scraped against the rock walls. One spark lit the weapons sack on fire, but Mel immediately smothered it. At the opening of the crevice the terrible lizards screamed and roared and scraped claws against stone, but it was no use. They were too large to follow.

The crevice turned into a very long passage, and the knights shuffled through it. Eventually it opened up into a craterlike area surrounded on all sides by steep rock walls.

The crevice appeared to be the only entrance. In the center of the crater was a peaceful lake, shimmering in the late-afternoon sun.

"We'll be safe here. It's hot. I suggest we have a swim to restore ourselves," said Erec.

He glanced at the Black Knight and Mel.

"Er, undertunics *on*. I think we all can agree."

The knights did agree. It was the first thing they had agreed on all day.

Mel, who was not a strong swimmer, opted to sit by the water's edge and organize the armor and weapons. She laid them out against the rocks.

The others stripped to their underthings and waded into the water.

It felt really, really good.

CHAPTER TEN

A CALM, COOL SWIM

The lake was large but not intimidatingly so. The knights floated, treaded water, and bobbed along contentedly.

Mel had cleaned the weapons and armor and set them in the sun to dry. She now paged through Merlin's book.

The knights, enjoying the quiet ripple of the lake, were silent.

"This reminds me of a pool near my home," said

Hector, finally. "I go there sometimes with my falcon."

"You are a falconer?" asked Bors. "So am I."

"Now a falcon is a predator I can get behind," said Erec, floating on his back.

"Their skill in hunting is quite admirable," said Magdalena.

"Strong claws," said Bors. "Could crush a man's hand. Well. Not mine, of course."

"They do have their whimsical side, too." Hector

chuckled. "They like shiny objects, just like ravens."

The conversation drifted into a pleasant silence.

"This is rather nice, fellow knights," said Erec. "Dare I say . . . peaceful?"

SPLASH!

The lake erupted beneath them as an enormous serpent broke the surface. Its neck was long. Its fins were massive. Its teeth were sharp. Life could certainly be unfair to the knights.

The serpent dived for Erec. Its neck swooped up before plunging down, teeth shining. But then it stopped in mid attack.

Bors was holding it by the neck.

The creature thrashed frantically. Its tail knocked Hector into the air, splashing him down a few yards away. He took a deep breath and swam underwater toward the belly of the beast.

The serpent reached back for Bors with its deadly jaws,

but the Black Knight burst out of the water beside it and grabbed its head.

Hector wrapped his arms around one flipper so it couldn't swim.

Erec climbed onto its back and pounded away with his fists.

The knights fought as one. There was no need for instruction. None swam to safety.

The serpent writhed with fury, knocking Bors, Hector, and Erec off.

But the Black Knight held tight, her grip like a steel vise, her focus singular and unshakable. The creature rolled, it leaped, it splashed, but nothing could shake the great knight.

Mel watched anxiously from the shore. Her mind raced. The weapons were too heavy for aquatic combat; besides, she'd never be able to throw a sword that far. But— *but*—

Mel grabbed a rock the size of her head.

At that very moment the Black Knight looked up.

Holding the serpent's neck with one arm, Magdalena lifted her other hand high.

Mel launched the rock with all of her might.

It sailed straight to Magdalena's hand, and in one smooth movement she brought it down on the serpent's head. The creature ceased its struggle instantly and sank below the surface, down to the depths.

The knights bobbed in the water, looking at one another.

They all nodded. It meant "nice work."

They began to swim to the shore.

Mel stood by the armor and weapons sack. The sun crept out from behind a cloud. The armor glistened brightly.

And that was when they heard the flapping sound.

Four gigantic flying lizards descended toward the shore in a flash. The knights swam faster, but it was no use. They watched helplessly as the flying creatures snatched the armor from the ground.

"Shiny . . . objects," sputtered Hector.

The flying lizards squawked and screeched. More came, each stealing away with the armor, the shields, the swords, the sack of weapons.

And Mel.

She struggled in the grip of the talons as she was carried up and away into the sky.

The knights reached shore and watched the flying lizards escape with everything except Merlin's book.

No one spoke.

Then Bors grabbed a large rock, gripping it in his massive fist until his knuckles were white. He started up the hill.

"Be he lad or lass," Bors growled, "no one steals *my* squire."

CHAPTER ELEVEN

SHINY OBJECTS

Mel had fainted. It was perhaps due to the height. Or maybe the ferocity and grip of the flying lizards. It could have been the sudden realization that all hope was lost. Any one of these things might cause a person to swoon. All combined? Fainting could hardly be helped.

She came to in an enormous nest made from hundreds of tree branches. A single flying lizard perched on a thick limb. The nest was so deep that when she stood, she was just able to see over the edge. But doing that was a mistake on two counts: one, it confirmed that the nest was perched on a very high mountain, and two, the flying lizard in the nest didn't seem to like her standing up without permission.

It screeched, and Mel's ears rang in pain. She sat back down. Beside her were various pieces of shining armor, swords, and the sack of extra weapons. Next to the sack was an enormous spotted egg.

Another flying lizard swooped down, its immense

wings generating a strong breeze. Mel flinched. The two fierce creatures stared at her. They blinked their beady eyes. But they did not attack. Mel was puzzled.

She looked at the egg beside her. She looked back at the flying lizards.

They looked at the egg and then looked at her.

Mel gulped.

She was baby's first meal.

Erec shaded his eyes as he stared up at the top of the mountain.

"That's the nest. I just saw her head poking out. She's still alive. But we'd better move fast."

He turned back. At the edge of some woods Bors, Hector, and Magdalena were pulling down thick, long vines.

"How's it coming?"

Bors tightened a knot of vines. He held up an end that had been looped into a lasso.

"It'll hold."

"Let's hope so, Sir Knight," said Erec. "Onward and upward."

Mel was trying to quiet the part of her brain that was filled with terrified screaming. She must think. She must find a way. This was the sort of thing she did. This was what she was good at. A squire was always thinking, planning, preparing.

Weapons. There are plenty of weapons, she thought.

One of the lizards hopped up suddenly. It landed again, perched close to the sack.

Okay, she thought. Perhaps not.

No! Be brave. She reached slowly for a sword.

The lizard snapped its beak and flapped its mighty wings.

Mel froze. Then she pulled back her hand and held it out to show that she was unfortunately without a weapon.

The knights ascended. They climbed steadily and in silence except for the occasional grunt. Erec took the lead. He tossed the lasso end of the vine up and around a jutting rock, secured it, and the others climbed up the makeshift rope after him. Then they repeated the process.

Climbing up to the next ledge, Bors reached for a crevice in the rock. He released his grip on the vine. The rock gave, and Bors fell.

His descent was short. Magdalena caught him with one powerful arm. She held the dangling Bors until he managed to grab hold of the vine once more.

He looked up at the Black Knight. He nodded.

She nodded.

They continued the ascent.

Mel wavered. She was feeling beaten. The flying lizards were too large. Too fast. Too attentive. It was hopeless.

But I mustn't give up, she thought. I have survived so far in this strange place. I have risked so much already, but—but—

Despair returned. *What* had she done exactly? Her days as a squire were over. She almost cried.

Almost.

But Melancholy Postlethwaite was made of sterner stuff. She would find a way. She just needed time.

At that moment the egg began to crack. A beak as long as Mel's arm poked through the shell. Mel looked up at the flying lizards. They were focused on her, their black eyes narrowing.

Finally the knights reached the ledge just below the nest. Magdalena coiled the long rope carefully and handed the lasso end to Erec.

"You throw it, Sir Erec. Your aim is best."

Erec took the vine.

Hector made room on the ledge for Bors to pass ahead of him.

"Sir Knight, you punch with far more accuracy than I. You go first."

"You are too kind, Sir Knight," said Bors.

Erec turned once more to his companions.

"Everyone know the plan?"

"Fight," said Hector.

"Get swords," said Magdalena.

"Then stab," said Bors.

"Splendid," said Erec.

The baby lizard broke free of the egg. The larger flying lizard spread its wings and shook them, readjusting its perch. The other opened its beak, revealing its razor teeth. It shrieked at Mel.

There was no time left. She inched her hand toward the nearest sword. Once she got it, she would fight with everything she had. She would not win, but she would die honorably. If only—

A lasso made of thick vine sailed over the side of the nest and landed beside her. Mel understood in an instant and quickly secured the rope to a large branch in the nest.

The lizards shifted and screamed. And then four Knights of the Round Table climbed onto the edge of the nest.

The knights roared and attacked. The flying lizards

shrieked and flapped into action. In a flash Mel supplied the knights with swords.

The baby lizard screamed out with hunger. Mel knew that the adult lizards would fight without mercy to protect their young. They needed an escape plan fast.

She found one. The vine!

Mel loosened the vine and pulled up the slack. She quickly threaded it through some helmets and armored breastplates. She secured the sack next, then attached the shields. She made a second lasso at the end of the vine.

Hector fought back one of the lizards. He checked on Mel and saw what she had done with the vine. The plan clicked. He grabbed one end of the rope.

Mel lassoed her end around the leg of the nearest flying lizard as it flapped its wings and lifted up. Hector did the same with the other end, attaching it neatly to the leg of the second flying lizard.

"Sir Knights!" shouted Mel. "Grab hold!"

The others joined Hector and Mel, gripping the vine. Soon enough the two flying lizards discovered that they were also attached to the strange rope. They were not amused. They rose higher in the air.

"Now!" shouted Erec.

The company, holding fast to the rope, leaped over the side of the nest. The flying lizards tried to escape, but they were connected by twenty feet of strong vine. More vexing still, the vine was weighted by armor, a sack of weapons, four knights, and their baby food.

The beasts flapped in vain, but they could only slow the descent. Down, down, down they glided.

As they neared the ground, Erec called out, "One. Two. Three!"

The knights let go of the vine and crashed safely into the dirt.

The Black Knight rolled and leaped up, sword held high. She sliced through the vine and the armor and sack slid off.

The furious creatures, free at last, rose swiftly. They screeched at their enemies but did not return.

The group all rose to their feet, dusting themselves off.

"Quick thinking, squire," said Erec. "I had frankly forgotten about an exit strategy."

"If there's one thing a squire knows, my lord," said Mel, "it's that armor and weaponry are rather heavy."

Hector and Magdalena patted Mel on the back and shoulder.

Bors nodded but said not a word.

CHAPTER TWELVE

COURT OF THE REX

The company traveled on. During a rest Hector paged through Merlin's book and made an important discovery about who, or what, the *Tyrannosaurus rex* actually was. He took the opportunity to educate the others. They all examined Merlin's book.

"Crikey, he's a big fellow," said Erec. "Clearly the king."

"Yes, it would appear to be the most terrible of the lizards."

"Let's go meet him then," said Bors, gathering up his sword and shield.

They climbed steadily up an incline. The trees were smaller and more bare. The air was thick. The noises were fewer.

The Black Knight stopped.

"I think we are getting close," she said.

The others joined her and saw what had stopped her in her tracks.

The skeleton of a three-horned beast lay before

them. Its bones were picked clean.

"There's another," said Bors, pointing down the trail to the remains of one of the long-necked creatures. "It's massive. And apparently no match for the king."

Farther along were several more skeletons, some intact, some torn to pieces. The path was strewn with carnage.

Hector gulped.

"Steady on," said Erec.

They moved slowly past the hulking skeletons and carcasses. Insects buzzed, and small scavenger lizards rustled past occasionally. Otherwise all was silent.

The bone trail led to a wide, dusty valley. Rock walls climbed up the western edge, and canyons and hills lay to the north. To the east was a tangled mass of dead gnarled trees and dry brush. The entire place felt like death. Nothing could thrive here.

Nothing except the king.

The knights entered the arena cautiously.

Mel pointed and spoke.

"There, on top of that rock hill. That's our cave."

It was indeed the cave. Their trek had brought them back to where they had started. But the hill leading to the cave was on the far side of the valley.

Rooooooaaaaaarrrrrr!

From the shadows of the valley an enormous creature emerged and blocked the path to the cave. Its powerful muscles rippled with each step. Its tail swished slowly in the air. Sharp teeth, too long to be contained, protruded from its mouth. Despite its size, it moved fast and carried itself with poise and confidence.

"Right," said Bors. "Not so bad."

Rocks crumbled underfoot. Two more tyrannosaurs joined the first. Each was bigger than the last. Finally the largest and most fearsome *Tyrannosaurus rex* of all took its place at the lead.

Hector's mouth hung open slightly.

"Oh. My. Lancelot."

"Looks like we have the entire royal family to deal with," said Erec.

"One for each," said Bors.

"No," said Erec. "We fight together. Mel, go to the side there in the brush. Make your way toward the cave once the battle begins. Stay low and stay quiet."

"Sir, I am not leaving," said Mel.

Erec turned to face her.

"We fight *together*. You said so yourself." Mel stood her ground.

"Very well. Now would be a good time for you to come up with another exit strategy. Stay alive at least until you think of something," said Erec with a grin.

The tyrannosaurs sniffed the air, snorted, and twitched their mighty tails.

The knights turned to face the terrible lizards. They drew their swords.

"Fellow knights," said Erec, "I would like to make a confession. In truth, I did not slay forty dragons.

Furthermore, I have never in my entire life even seen a dragon."

There was silence.

"Neither have I," stated Bors.

"Nor I," said Hector.

"Not one," said Magdalena.

"But here, in this strange land, we have encountered the fiercest, most terrible creatures imaginable," Erec continued. "And time and again we, valiant knights, fought bravely and well. We have matched them in strength and courage, and we have bested them in strategy." He nodded to Mel.

Mel nodded back.

"I say this not as a boast. It is the truth. Our deeds have no need for embellishment or exaggeration." Erec paused. "I have no illusions about what we now face. These monsters may very well be the end of us. They are certainly worthy opponents."

The largest T-rex took a step toward the knights.

"But we are Knights of King Arthur's Round Table.

This is a glorious day, and I cannot imagine being among a better band of heroes."

Shields raised, swords at the ready, the four knights strode toward the terrible lizards.

The tyrannosaurs attacked in a flash. The shields were no match for the force of the initial impact, and the knights were knocked back.

Erec swung at the belly of one beast. His sword glanced off the thick hide but did not pierce it.

No one's swords could penetrate the terrible lizards' armor. Bors, mace in one hand, sword in the other, attacked in a fierce combination of blows and stabs.

But the teeth and jaws were the real danger. The lizards were fast and furious, and their chomps brutal and nonstop.

Erec was the first to find himself lifted several feet off the ground. His armor kept the teeth from puncturing his vital organs, but the pressure of the monster's bite was tremendous. He whacked the terrible lizard on the snout. And then he whacked again. And again.

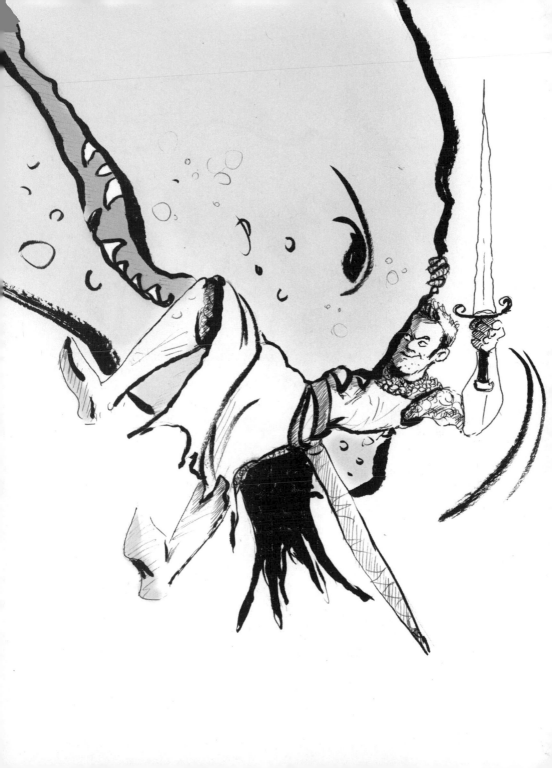

Sir Hector dodged the stomping legs of another tyrannosaur, pivoted, and brought his sword down on the tail of Erec's captor. The monster spun and loosened its grip enough for Erec to slip out and grab hold of its neck.

Its mercifully tiny arms reached and clawed, but to no avail. Erec kicked his leg against the beast's chest and flipped up onto its back. He gouged its eyes from behind.

Hector and Bors stood back-to-back, facing off against two opponents. The flurry of swords kept the beasts at bay but not deterred. They attacked with relentless energy.

When Erec was finally tossed from the bucking tyrannosaur, he landed harshly on the ground and rolled away just in time to avoid being squashed underfoot.

The Black Knight, sword in hand, fought back the largest of the tyrannosaurs. She saw Erec, badly winded with a T-rex ready to pounce on him. Erec struggled to his feet. His opponent snorted and slowly opened its jaws, saliva dripping to the ground.

Magdalena turned back to the gigantic T-rex and shoved a sword into its mouth, lodging the weapon in its jaws. As the monster struggled, she leaped onto its tremendous haunch and hoisted herself onto its back. She took a deep breath. And then, with amazing dexterity, she ran straight down the T-rex's spine, out onto the tail, and leaped off the monster just as the other T-rex launched itself at Erec.

The Black Knight landed between Erec and the beast. In a flash she lifted a discarded shield and blocked the creature. Erec got to his feet and threw a mace to the

Black Knight. Magdalena caught it and dealt the T-rex a mighty blow.

Mel watched in horror from the trees. The knights fought bravely—braver than any before surely—but the odds were against them. The tyrannosaurs did not stop. They would not stop.

She pulled the sack of extra weapons toward her. She might need to supply new weapons at a moment's notice—

Notice. Notice!

Her hand was gripping the bit of burned sack that had caught fire in the crevice by the lake. *Fire*. Mel dug into her pouch for her flint and striking stone. After several frantic moments a spark caught a dead tree branch. She blew the flame, and it rose and licked its way up the wood.

Mel waved the branch like a torch. Running along the edge of the arena, she spread the blaze. It wound through the dry brush to the hill where the cave was located.

"Sir Knights!" she yelled.

Those who could looked up. Unfortunately so did one of the terrible lizards. It roared in her direction. Then it charged. But Sir Bors launched himself into the air and brought his sword down on the monster's foot. It snarled and turned, teeth bared. Bors bared his own teeth and roared back. He swung one powerful fist in a precisely placed uppercut. The punch connected.

The terrible lizard's eyes crossed; it wobbled on its injured foot, then toppled over with a tremendous THUD.

Bors snorted and turned, fists ready.

"Go!" he yelled at Mel.

She ran, spreading the fire, which burned higher and higher.

Hector and Erec swung their swords at their foes,

knocking them back with each powerful blow. Soon Hector turned and ran toward the wall of flame. He bolted through a small opening in the blaze to join Mel. Erec came next, crashing through the fire. He stopped, dropped, and rolled on the ground to extinguish some stray flames.

Eventually Bors leaped through the fire to join the others at the foot of the hill. Three of the tyrannosaurs approached the line slowly, the inferno confusing and angering them. They roared. They chomped the fire, then recoiled in pain. The barrier was working.

"Where is the Black Knight?" said Mel, throwing her torch into the blaze.

The knights peered through the flames and smoke.

"There!" shouted Bors.

The Black Knight faced off with the tyrant king. They slowly circled each other. The king swished its tail and snarled. It snapped at her. She jumped away, landed, then attacked, bringing down her mace. The handle broke in two. Magdalena tossed it aside. There were no other weapons within reach. She ran for the fire line.

"Quickly!" called Erec.

The Black Knight stumbled and fell. The king was on her in an instant, snapping her up in its jaws, her armor creaking and groaning. She pushed at its upper jaw, but the powerful beast clamped down even harder.

That was when she got mad.

The Black Knight grabbed a single tooth and pulled and pulled and tore it right out of the king's gum. It opened its mouth in a roar of pain. The Black Knight took hold of the king's tongue, yanked it out, and swung to the ground.

Perhaps the king of the terrible lizards had never felt such a sensation. For a moment it didn't appear to know *what* to do, which was enough time for the Black Knight to race for the fire line again. She jumped straight through and landed safely on the other side.

The king stuck its enormous head through the flames, then pulled back with a roar. The terrible lizards panicked.

Smoke filled the clearing. As long as the fire around them raged, they were trapped.

"Ha-ha!" Erec chortled. "I'll bet they wish they were dragons *now*, eh?"

Bors slapped Erec heartily on the back.

"Good line, Sir Erec! Very witty indeed!"

And with that the company made a hasty climb up the hill to the cave.

CHAPTER THIRTEEN

THE END OF
THE ADVENTURE

With the fire keeping the *Tyrannosaurus rex* family at bay far below, the knights and Mel entered the cave and strode down the passageway to the book chamber.

"Hear us, Merlin!" said Erec in his most booming voice. "We have bested the tyrant king of the terrible lizards and herewith request our reward. Return us to England!"

A strong wind blew through the dark cave, then stopped suddenly.

Erec strode back to the entrance. He looked out.

"Ah, vermin! Didn't work."

A tremendous roar from somewhere below confirmed this to the rest of the company.

"Perhaps Merlin's book could help," Mel suggested.

Hector placed the book on the rock at the center of the chamber. He paged to the end.

"Oh, there appears to be a note. I shall read it aloud for you."

Hector cleared his throat. And then cleared his throat again.

"Oh, just read it already, Hector," said Bors.

Dear Knights,

I have detailed the aspects of the Terrible Lizards in these pages for your quiet perusal. However, it is likely you have ignored this volume entirely and ventured out to see for yourselves. I hope that worked out for you. And if there are any of you left and you still have heads, let alone eyes to read these words, I do hope you will reflect on your experience.

Terrible and magnificent creatures have indeed walked this earth. Perhaps they still do or will again one day. I hope that you now have a proper amount of respect for these fierce beasts and that this knowledge may help curb your more boastful assertions of knightly bravery and exploits.

And now my enchanted owl is tired and requests that I dictate no more for him to inscribe. Fare-thee-well or farewell, Brave Knights (whichever is the case).

Best,

Merlin

The knights looked at one another.

"Has this"—Erec began slowly and evenly—"has this

entire adventure just been one of Merlin's Teachable Moments?"

"Yes, I believe so," said Hector. "Furthermore, it appears that we could have simply sat here and *read the book*."

There was a long silence.

"Well, where would the fun be in that?" said Magdalena.

More silence.

Until a chuckle came from Bors. Soon Erec joined in. And Hector. And Mel. Magdalena smiled a rare smile, and then, even more extraordinary, she laughed.

The whole cave echoed with laughter.

And then four torches blazed.

The knights walked to the entrance and looked out.

"Merry ol' England," said Erec.

Indeed it was. There were fine trim oaks. The woods were orderly and proper. A squirrel hurried by. It wasn't even a large squirrel.

The knights descended the hill. They found their horses just as they had left them, grazing peacefully in the shade. The knights went to their steeds.

"One moment," said Bors, placing a hand gently on Mel's shoulder.

"Mel," he said. It was the first time he had ever used her name. "You have acted with cunning and bravery. Your contribution to this quest is undeniable."

Mel glowed. Warmth radiated through her. She stood a little taller.

"But—"

It was one small word. Yet her face looked as though Sir Bors had thrust a sword through her.

"I am afraid that I cannot have a girl as a squire. It just . . . it just isn't done."

He held out his hand. Mel knew what it meant, knew there was no argument to be made.

She handed Bors the sack of weapons that she had so dutifully carried.

He took it and secured it to the weapons horse. Then he mounted his own horse and set off, pulling the reins of the weapons horse behind him.

Erec and Hector each gazed at Mel silently, but then followed Bors on the path to Camelot.

Mel stood there alone. Small. Lost.

Until a shadow fell over her. She turned.

The Black Knight was beside her, high on her midnight steed.

"Come with me, if you like. Be whoever you wish to be."
She lowered a hand. "A good squire is a good squire."

Mel smiled. She reached up, and the Black Knight easily lifted her onto the back of the horse.

They rode on without another word.

That evening the four knights returned to Camelot and the court of King Arthur.

They waited until all were assembled in the great hall. Especially Merlin. This entrance had to count.

The massive oak doors opened with a bit of tasteful fanfare. The Knights of the Round Table turned in unison.

Sir Erec, Sir Bors, Sir Hector, and the Black Knight strode in, still wearing their battle-scarred armor.

A hush fell over the hall.

Merlin sat up straight, a small inscrutable smile under his long beard.

"Approach," said Arthur.

Sir Erec strode before the king and queen and bowed.

"Sire, we have returned from battling the terrible

lizards. They were indeed fearsome, more so than any dragon in existence, but"—Erec looked back at his fellow knights—"*together* we bested them all."

"Step forward, all of you," said Arthur.

Hector and Bors approached and bowed. The Black Knight remained in the shadows, helmet and visor on as usual.

Arthur waited.

"All of you, I said." Arthur's voice was quiet, but that meant that he was really, really serious.

The Black Knight came forward. And for the first time in Camelot she removed her helmet. Magdalena bowed.

There were gasps. A few forks dropped out of the hands of stunned knights. Wine was spit out in surprise.

Arthur cleared his throat. Guinevere tilted her head slightly. Merlin merely nibbled on some lettuce. He didn't seem particularly surprised.

Erec broke the silence.

"Your Majesty, I know this is highly . . . irregular. But I must tell you and all here at court that before you stands the bravest and mightiest knight I have ever known.

"Sorry, Lancelot," Erec added quickly.

Lancelot waved it off. Little things didn't bother him.

"Your name?" asked Arthur.

"Magdalena, sire. Daughter of Robert the Blacksmith."

Arthur considered this for a moment.

"Very well, Black Knight."

Everyone exhaled.

"Join us for a feast, brave knights. Tell your tale. Teach the minstrels some new songs," said Arthur. "For all our sakes."

"Gladly, sire," said Erec. "But first—"

He glanced at Magdalena. She grinned. Magdalena

tossed something into the air, and Erec caught it without looking.

"My queen, we have brought a trophy for you and our king."

Erec held up an enormous tooth, a souvenir from the great *Tyrannosaurus rex*.

Guinevere took the tooth. Merlin's eyebrows rose with interest.

"Well, well done, brave Knights," said Guinevere. "A most terrible lizard indeed."

Erec bowed low.

The formalities completed, the hall once again filled with chatter, music, and excitement. Bors and Hector held various knights spellbound. Lancelot engaged in his first conversation with the Black Knight, who in truth, he had long admired. Even Mel was surrounded by the other squires in the antechamber of the great hall.

Minstrels were summoned, and they began to compose new and exciting songs.

Sir Erec, however, took his leave quietly and walked alone to the great door of the hall. His tunic was slightly scratchy. He was very tired.

The adventure was over, and his bed awaited.

CHAPTER FOURTEEN

BAND OF SIBLINGS

Erec slept deeply and soundly and free of dreams. He awoke to a breeze wafting into his bedchamber. A few songbirds twittered pleasantly nearby. He yawned. He was content.

Then the clatter of fallen armor rang through the outer rooms. After a timid knock the door opened a crack. Derek the squire poked his long nose into the chamber.

"Sir Erec?" he whispered.

"What is it, Derek? It had better be eggs and bacon."

"Um, not quite, my lord."

"Come in, squire."

The squire entered, holding a scroll of parchment.

"This arrived early this morning, Sir Erec, but I didn't want to wake you."

"Hand it here."

Derek did so and stood at attention.

Erec read silently. He rolled the parchment up.

He sighed.

"It seems," he said, getting out of bed, "that King Arthur has been so inspired by our magnificent adventure that he has proposed a new quest to all of the Knights of the Round Table."

He brushed Derek aside, grabbed some clothes, and swept through the door. Derek scurried after him.

"He wants us to search for the Holy Grail."

Erec put on his chain mail shirt and tunic.

"What on earth is the Holy Grail you may be wondering, my dear squire. Well, I'll tell you." He continued in a louder, slightly annoyed voice.

"It is a legendary item, lost for centuries, quite possibly not even in existence."

He fastened his belt and stepped into his boots.

"No clues, no leads. All of the earth to cover"—he threw open the front door—"in a search that is sure to be time-consuming and exceedingly dangerous."

There in the courtyard awaited Sir Hector, Sir Bors, and the Black Knight, all suited and ready, magnificent in their clawed and bitten armor and sitting on their finest horses. Mel was there, too, dressed smartly in black, riding a white horse behind the Black Knight. She held a new banner that showed a field of red with the silhouette of a terrible lizard at the center, surrounded by four swords. The same symbol decorated the shield of each knight.

"What an absolutely splendid idea." Sir Erec smiled.

A NOTE
FROM
MERLIN

Many of the terrible lizards (otherwise known as dinosaurs) in this tale did not truly walk the earth during the same eras or in the same regions. But didn't our heroes deserve the most epic battles? I thought that a more generous sampling of creatures from the ages might be more illuminating and entertaining for the knights.

Here are a few interesting facts about some of the dinosaurs in this book:

SPINOSAURUS

The Spinosaurus lived in the Cretaceous period, between 112 million and 97 million years ago. It was a carnivore, which means it ate meat. It had long spines forming a sail along its back. It was the biggest of all carnivorous dinosaurs and lived on both land and water, much like a modern-day crocodile.

TRICERATOPS

The Triceratops lived during the end of the Cretaceous period, about 68 million to 66 million years ago. It was an herbivore, which means it ate plants. The triceratops had three big horns on its skull and was about the size of an African elephant.

Ankylosaurus

The Ankylosaurus lived during the end of the Cretaceous period as well, about 70 million to 66 million years ago. It was an herbivore. It is known as one of the most heavily armored lizards because of the hard knobs and oval plates of bone that formed within its skin, such as what's found on crocodiles, armadillos, and modern lizards. It had a large club at the end of its tail thought to be used for self-defense.

Brachiosaurus

The Brachiosaurus lived during the late Jurassic to early Cretaceous periods, about 150 million to 130 million years ago. It was an herbivore. Its long neck allowed it to reach tall trees and vegetation not available to other animals. The Brachiosaurus could reach vegetation up to 39 feet off the ground and could eat up to 600 pounds of plant matter a day.

ELASMOSAURUS PLATYURUS

The Elasmosaurus platyurus lived during the Cretaceous period, about 80 million years ago. It was a carnivore. The Elasmosaurus platyurus was a marine reptile, with four long, paddle-like flippers that it used to swim slowly, similarly to turtles. It had a short tail, but a very long neck, with as many as 75 vertebrae in its neck alone.

TYRANNOSAURUS REX

Tyrannosaurus rex lived during the late Cretaceous period, between 68 million and 66 million years ago. It was a carnivore, and ate mostly herbivorous dinosaurs. The Tyrannosaurus rex had a massive jaw and a strong bite—stronger than any other land animal that has ever lived. The largest Tyrannosaurus rex tooth ever recorded was twelve inches long.

DIP
DIP
DIP

What mayhem is hiding from our
heroes in the magical mist?
Read on for a frightfully exciting
excerpt from

KNIGHTS
VS.
MONSTERS

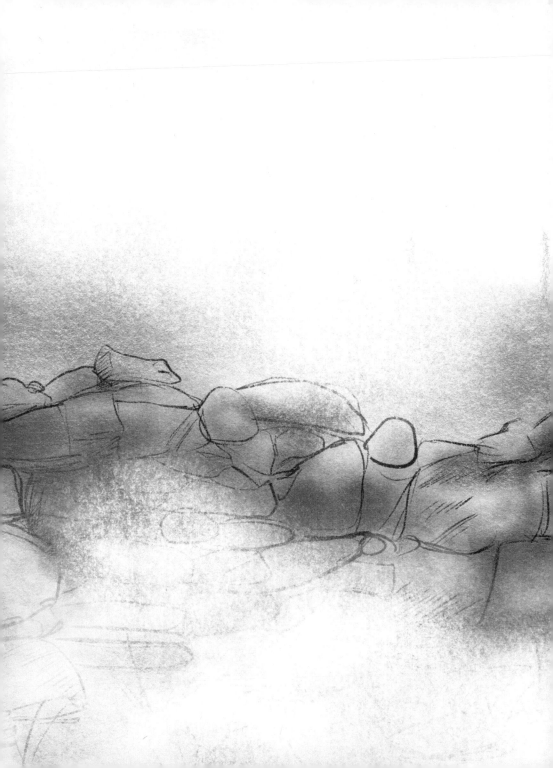

PROLOGUE

Something lurked in the mist. Something large. Something nasty.

Four knights and one young girl stumbled half blind on the dark, misty moor as well.

"Where is it?" yelled Sir Erec of the Round Table, brandishing his broadsword. "BORS!"

Sir Bors bounded out of the mist, swinging his sword every which way. "There's more than one! Where's Hector?"

"I don't know. Can't see anything in this blasted mist."
Erec turned sharply. "There! I think—"

He didn't finish the sentence. An enormous hairy arm with fiendish claws burst from the mist and sliced Erec's garment.

Bors raised his blade with a deep battle cry. Erec regained his footing and joined the battle.

"Hector! We need you! NOW!" he called.

Elsewhere . . .

Magdalena, the Black Knight, moved slowly, cautiously, a sword in one hand, a dagger in the other. Her eyes, intense and piercing, scanned the impenetrable fog.

She took a single breath.

An enormous tentacle whipped through the mist and wrapped around her legs, knocking her to the ground. She dropped her sword but still held the knife. The Black Knight slashed at the tentacle but could not quite reach it.

The tentacle dragged her across the rocky terrain. A low growl rumbled louder and louder.

Suddenly . . .

An arrow pierced the tentacle. The mysterious beast roared.

Melancholy Postlethwaite leaped from behind a stone wall, a bow in hand, a fresh arrow released in midair.

Mel landed, rolled, sprang to her feet, and helped the Black Knight untangle from the flailing tentacle. But seven more whipped furiously above them. The Black Knight found her sword, drew herself to her full intimidating height, and wiped a strand of hair from her eyes. Mel stood beside her, bow at the ready.

Meanwhile . . .

Bors and Erec soared backward through the air and landed with a thud against a small stone hut.

Winded, they slowly rallied their strength.

The sound of enormous feet crunched toward them.

They froze, eyes on the dark mist. A monster emerged from the gloom. It was huge, terrifying, fierce, and—

"Wait," said Erec. "Is that a wee mustache?"

In a darkened hall of Camelot, two court minstrels sat by a small fire, tuning their instruments.

"That's not it," said the first. "He shouted: 'We must act!'"

"No, it was 'wee mustache.'"

"That doesn't make any sense."

The minstrel shrugged. "That's the most reliable tale at the moment. Some Scottish peasant came through town the other day. He'd heard the tale from a cousin of a cousin who was there and sent a letter all about it via raven. I heard it from John Muddle, the tinsmith. Who told you?"

"Bertha, the innkeeper. But that's exactly the problem, you see. It's all hearsay. Worse, it's whisper-down-the-lane. How is a respectable minstrel expected to know all the little details?"

"We do what we can, Paul."

They continued tuning.

"I hear the squire is now quite an accomplished archer."

"Well, that's what I mean, John. You *hear*? From whom?"

"Lionel. Lutist from . . . Devon, I think."

"Ugh. What a hack."

"I know. But he has a new song called 'Melancholy the Erstwhile Squire Who Is Now an Accomplished Archer.'"

"Good title. But Lionel has no sense of melody."

"Tell me about it. And how difficult is basic song structure? Verse, verse, verse, verse, verse, verse, verse, chorus, repeat."

The fire crackled. A string twanged into tune.

"I wonder where he heard the archer bit."

"Who knows? We won't have the full accurate account, the *actual* facts of the story, until the Band of the Terrible Lizards returns."

"They shan't return."

A dark figure emerged from the shadows of the hall.

"Sir Gawain. We did not see you there."

Gawain stood by the fire and poked it slowly. "I have just received word from my brother, Sir Agravaine. Grave news from our home." Gawain put the poker down and stared at the blazing fire for a moment. "The Band of the Terrible Lizards has met their end. They fought bravely, of course. . . . "

He turned and walked to the door of the hall.

"But some things are unconquerable, even for the greatest of heroes."

Mel and the Oozing 'Orror

Magdalena and the Rabid Rapscallion

Hector and the Fingers of Fear

Bors and the Boarish Beast

Exec and the Eel of Misery

Books by
MATT PHELAN

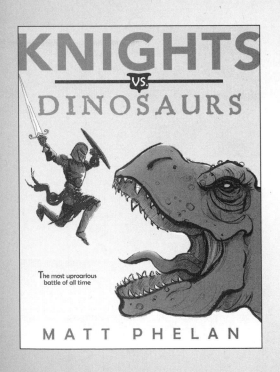

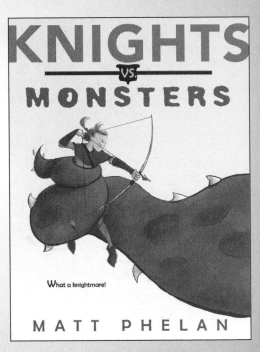